"He's a pioneer and those in the speech and voice field should pay attention." ------Dennis Weaver

"After I retired from the ring, I stepped into a world of broadcasting and commercials. Thanks to Dr. Cooper, I have a second career. Dr. Cooper's a voice champ."
------Carlos Palomino,
Former World Welterweight Champion

"Can put magic into almost any voice."
------Richard Crenna

"Cooper's approach is the way to go." ------John Saxon

"You gave me back my voice. . . . Your approach to vocal rehabilitation, I am convinced, is the most advanced and effective there is." ------Cantor Richard Allen,
Director of Music, Keneseth Israel Temple,
Philadelphia, Pennsylvania

"It was like a miracle pain reliever. Dr. Cooper said: 'Here's a quick and easy end to those voice nightmares.' My voice was becoming strangled; I was losing control of my range and my tone. After years of discomfort, tension and stress, after studying with numerous voice coaches and suffering endless debilitating bimonthly throat infections, in a flash, almost overnight, Dr. Cooper's techniques changed my whole approach to using my voice. Almost by magic, my voice problems disappeared. It was astoundingly, hilariously simple and logical and it worked." ------Shadoe Stevens
TV/Radio Personality and Producer

"Superb." ------Werner Erhard

"In 30 seconds or less, Dr. Morton Cooper gave me a younger and healthier voice. Need I say more?"

------Milo Frank, Author of
How to Get Your Point Across in 30 Seconds or Less

"It's really miraculous."   ------Norton Simon,
Norton Simon Industries,
Wall Street Journal

". . . The McEnroe of voice coaches. . ."   ------Rob Lowe

"A gifted voice coach. . . . Every season and every summer at camp I used to lose my voice. Mort Cooper taught me how to project my voice. . . I have not lost my voice in two years. It has been a tremendous relief. I believe in him."   ------Jim Harrick
UCLA Basketball Coach

". . . enabled me to expand my vocal range."
------Cheryl Ladd

"He added 20 years to my vocal career."
------Jerome Hines,
Metropolitan Opera Star

"Fantastic."   ------Roosevelt Grier

"Dr. Cooper is terrific. He has done wonders with my voice. Now if he can only do something with the other parts of my body."   ------Jan Murray,
Comedian

"Dr. Cooper put me on the right track --- for a better voice."   ------Jackie Joyner Kersee,
Olympic Gold Medalist

"Finally! I've found someone who knows what they're doing -- he made my voice come alive -- it now has so much color -- the answer to my prayers!

"I walked into his office with a thin nasal voice and am walking out with a sultry, sexy, resonant voice. He's wonderful!"   ------Sela Ward

"Your techniques work wonders. . . . it's like a miracle!"
                                    ------The Reverend James Johnson
                                    Poplar Grove, Illinois

"Almost overnight Dr. Cooper turned my career around."
                                    ------Ciji Ware
                                    KABC Commentator and Author

"Morton Cooper saved my voice. . . and made me a lot of money with my voice by teaching me to use it properly. It took less time than flying from L.A. to Chicago and it was a lot more fun."   ------Stanley Ralph Ross, Ph.D.
                                    Author, Entertainer

"After just an hour with Dr. Cooper, I noticed a change in my voice, and I had a direction to go in. It's so simple, it's phenomenal."   ------O. J. Simpson

"The results of my intensive therapy with Dr. Cooper bordered on the miraculous."   ------Dr. Ellis Rivkin
                                    Adolph S. Ochs Professor of Jewish History
                                    Hebrew Union College,
                                    Cincinnati, Ohio

"Mort Cooper is a voice computer genius. Finding a new method to help people to discover the innate power of their own voices and speech has made him the foremost speech therapist in the world."   ------Harold Robbins,
                                    Best Selling Author

"He saved my voice and my career. He is the Master Voice Wizard."
------Jim Herbert, Esq.
Chairman, Barpassers Review

"Morton Cooper's therapy restored my voice. Without, it would have changed my life for the worse. He is a superb therapist."
------Alfred Gottschalk, Ph.D., Rabbi
President, Hebrew Union College,
Cincinnati, Ohio

"He turned my whole life around."
------Marjorie Whitman
Homemaker

WHAT THE EXPERTS HAVE SAID . . .
ABOUT DR. MORTON COOPER

"Dr. Morton Cooper has shown unusual expertise in treating patients with spasmodic dysphonia. His methods of voice therapy in our patients afflicted with this markedly disabling disease have been highly successful."

------Edward Kantor, M.D.
Chairman, Division of Otolaryngology,
Head and Neck Surgery, Cedars-Sinai Medical Center

Of Spasmodic Dysphonia, Dr. Rubin said, "We know you are the only one successful by speech therapy."
Of all Voice Disorders, Dr. Rubin said, "Dr. Cooper's methods seemed essentially quite simple, but they worked."   ------Henry J. Rubin, M.D., Retired
UCLA School of Medicine, Head & Neck Division

"Dr. Cooper is the best speech pathologist I know."

------Joel Pressman, M.D.
Former Chairman of the Head & Neck Division,
UCLA Medical Center

"He's the best in the business."

------Lee Edward Travis, Ph.D.
A Founder and Past President of the American
Speech-Language-Hearing Assoc. (ASHA)

"Before you think of surgery, think of Dr. Cooper's 'magic' cure; it even astounds the doctors."

------Gershon Lesser, M.D.
Host of "The Health Connection"

"I found him to be really excellent. . . ."

------Robert H. Rand, Ph.D., M.D.
Professor of Neurological Surgery,
UCLA Medical Center

STOP
COMMITTING
VOICE
SUICIDE

DR. MORTON COOPER

Voice & Speech Company of America   Los Angeles

NOTE: Although most of the names have been changed to protect the privacy of the individuals involved, the case histories are factual.

Library of Congress Cataloging in Publication Data

Library of Congress Catalog Card Number: 95-062223

Cooper, Morton, 1931-
  Stop committing voice suicide.

  1. Voice culture. I. Title
PN4162. C 65   1996   808.5
ISBN 0-87980-437-8   (pbk.)

Printed in the United States of America

Contents

Talking Without Air
"Poison is a Poor Choice"
Seek Options . . . Not the Easy Cure
Freeing the Patient from Medical Dependency

3 De-Mystify and De-Medicalize

From Doctor to Doctor . . . to Doctor
Ready to Give Up
"It's a Nuthouse Out There . . ."
A Voice Mystery
The Profit Game
Band-Aid Treatments
Additional Cover-Up Treatments
The Thyroid Gland
Published Findings
Surgical Ramifications
Thyroplasty

4 All the Presidents' Voices

The Up-and-Down Voices of the Presidents
The Voice of FDR
Truman's "Give 'em Hell" Sound
Ike's Little Known Voice Problem
JFK: A Voice Unrealized
LBJ's Troubled Voice
Nixon: Potential Gone Awry
Ford's "Nightmare"
Carter: A Voice with Few Listeners
Reagan: The Most Trusted Voice in America
Bush: No Sound Impression
Clinton's Voice: A Medical Controversy
The Presence of Great Speakers

5 Voice Suicide: Whatever Happened to Voices?

Star Quality Voices
The Importance of Voice Help
Voice Suicide
Hearing Yourself Talk
Role Playing in Voice

Danger Signals: The Dirty Little Secrets of the
Sexual Speaking Voice
The "Confidential" Voice
A Personal Experience
How Voices Develop
Seeking Competent Voice Help

What's Going On?
A Voice in the Wilderness?

Introduction

In *Stop Committing Voice Suicide,* Dr. Cooper spotlights the symptoms of troubled voices and presents amazing voice discoveries — simple, safe, and natural ways to help these voices or to improve the speaking and/or singing voice. Dr. Cooper provides a direction, an orientation to assist people in voice care which is based on extensive clinical practice.

This book tells why our voices are poor and troubled. Most of us basically have good voices, but we seldom realize it. More often than not, we suffer from misuse and abuse of our voices because we have no real direction on the use of our speaking voice. The prevalence of troubled or failing voices is of epidemic, but unrecognized, proportions.

Dr. Cooper observes that we have a range of notes that we seldom utilize effectively. He finds about fifty percent of the population talk too child-like, too nasal, too high pitched, too whiny; about twenty-five percent talk deep-throat, with the tone centered about the level of the vocal cords. Our breathing is shallow, reversed or without control, so that we are exhausted or tired from talking after relatively short periods of time.

These bad voice habits, or speaking incorrectly, create negative voice symptoms. Common symptoms include a tired, weak voice, voice fatigue, throat clearing, coughing, a hoarse, raspy, or guttural voice, throat tension, pain when talking, loss of voice, laryngitis, continued sore throat without medical cause, reduced voice range, voice not heard or understood, a child-like voice which lacks authority in an adult, a nasal sound, a "lump in the throat" feeling (also called a "frog in the throat"), a foggy voice in the morning.

Dr. Cooper's description of our voices and voice rehabilitation allows the reader to realize that voices are what we make of them. "Hopeless" voices are not necessarily hopeless. The treatment of one particular disorder, the strangled voice, known medically as spasmodic dysphonia, is discussed. Dr. Cooper offers hope, finding that this voice problem, as well as many other troubled voices, is usually caused from talking incorrectly, not from genes, neurological causes, environment, diet, reflux, dehydration, sinusitis, postnasal drip or allergy. Today, many in the medical field seem to be of the view that reflux is a major cause of voice disorders instead of voice misuse and/or abuse.

In this book, Dr. Cooper surveys Presidential voices from Roosevelt through Clinton, underscoring the importance of voice in Presidential campaigns, past and present. Other chapters cover the voices of children and adults, speaking and singing voices, problems and solutions. A segment of this book discusses the problem of stuttering and the recovery of normal speech through a better voice and through awareness of what constitutes normal speech.

Dr. Cooper observes that all too many people come to his office after they have tried everything else and realize nothing has worked. Yet time after time, he is able to help them recover a normal voice by Direct Voice Rehabilitation — a system that treats simply, directly, naturally, and holistically the basic attributes of voices and provides an alternative approach to treatment of voice disorders.

Acknowledgements

I am indebted to a number of patients present and past for their insights and experiences. I thank them for their kindness and permission to relate their concerns to a wider audience.

To all the celebrities who have allowed me to use their names, who gave me quotes, and who let me tell their stories, I am forever grateful.

I thank in particular Fred Basten for helping express my literary voice as well as for his constant good humor, endless patience and enduring kindness.

I also want to express my appreciation to others who assisted in the formulation of this book, specifically:

Special recognition and thanks to attorneys Ronald Litz and Jennifer Litz for the benefit of their legal expertise, support, compassion, and sense of truth and justice.

Muriel Paule for her editorial review and critique of the manuscript.

Melvin Powers for his advice concerning the book.

Mark L. Burgio for the book cover design and the drawing of diagrams.

Andrea Burke for her secretarial assistance.

Lorna Cooper for her excellent word processing skills which she applied to this manuscript.

Lorna Cooper and Marla Cooper for listening, reading, and making suggestions about the book.

Marcia Hartung Cooper, M.A. for bringing to life, *Stop Committing Voice Suicide*.

About the Author

A nationally-acclaimed voice and speech clinician, Dr. Morton Cooper is regarded as a pioneer in the areas of voice training, voice improvement, and voice rehabilitation. He has been in private practice in the fields of voice, speech, and language rehabilitation for thirty years.

Dr. Cooper is the author of *Change Your Voice, Change Your Life* (a best-selling book now in the 15th printing) and *Winning With Your Voice* , both of which present ways of improving your speaking voice. Other books include the widely acclaimed *Modern Techniques of Vocal Rehabilitation* and is co-editor (with his wife) of *Approaches to Vocal Rehabilitation.* Dr. Cooper's work has been included in the *Handbook of Speech Pathology and Audiology,* edited by Lee Travis; in *Current Pediatric Therapy* , edited by S. S. Gellis and B. M. Kagan; and *Great Singers on Great Singing* by Jerome Hines. Dr. Cooper has written more than ninety articles and columns on voice, speech, and language disorders which have appeared in many leading national publications.

Dr. Cooper has appeared on numerous national television talk shows, including *Oprah, CNN, Good Morning America, The Today Show, The Merv Griffin Show, Hour Magazine, The Regis Philbin Show, The 700 Club, The E Entertainment Network, The Sonya Show, Sonya Friedman Live, Nightwatch, Late Night America, The Joe Franklin Show,* and *The Financial News Network,* among others. He was featured on the television show, *The Crusaders,* where he reported recoveries and cures with the strangled voice, medically known as spasmodic dysphonia. Dr. Cooper has also appeared on a number of local television shows across the United States. He has been heard on many radio shows, including Larry King, Michael Jackson, Ray Briem, and Owen Spann.

Many writers have interviewed Dr. Cooper about his voice rehabilitation techniques; these interviews have appeared in *The Los Angeles Times, The Wall Street Journal, The Washington Post, USA Today, US Magazine, Mademoiselle, Self, Prevention,* and *The New York Times Sunday Magazine.* Dr. Cooper's own writings (studies, articles, papers, and columns) have been printed in the *Journal of Speech and Hearing Disorders, California Medicine, Archives of Otolaryngology, Medical Tribune, Pediatric News, Eye, Ear, Nose and Throat Monthly, Journal of Communication Disorders, Journal of Fluency Disorders, Wall Street Journal, Cosmopolitan, Let's Live, Advance, Voices: The Art and Science of Psychotherapy, Geriatrics, Grade Teacher, Education, United Teacher, Peabody Journal of Education, Bulletin of the National Association of Teachers of Singing, Voice, Music Educators Journal, Prevention, Bar Bulletin, Case and Comment, Trial, Screen Actor,* and *The Quill.*

Dr. Cooper has a B.A. from Brooklyn College, an M.A. from Indiana University, and a Ph.D. from UCLA. He was formerly the Director of Voice and Speech Pathology, Outpatient Clinic, and a Clinical Assistant Professor, Head and Neck Surgery Division, UCLA Center for the Health Sciences. Prior to this, he was Director of the Adult Stutterers' Group at Stanford University. He has taught In-Service classes for the Los Angeles City Schools, and extension courses for UCLA

Medical Center and for UCLA Extension Division. He has been a consultant and a regular speaker at the Pritikin Longevity Center.

Dr. Cooper has been a speaker for numerous organizations, among which are the American Telemarketing Association, the American Cancer Society, the American Theatre Association, the National Association of Teachers of Singing, MENSA, the Los Angeles Bar Association, and the Los Angeles Book Club. He has addressed many groups at medical facilities, including UCLA Medical Center, Cedars-Sinai Medical Center, St. John's Hospital, Walter Reed Army Hospital, White Memorial Medical Center, Kaiser-Permanente Hospital, the Los Angeles Society of Otolaryngology, the Los Angeles Neurological Society, the Ross-Loos Medical Group, and the California Dental Association.

Dr. Cooper is licensed as a Speech Pathologist in California, and he is certified in Speech Pathology by the American Speech-Language-Hearing Association (ASHA). He has received a certificate of appreciation from ASHA that states: "In recognition of a significant contribution to the American Speech-Language-Hearing Association and to the profession of speech pathology and audiology."

1

The Shocking Truth About Voices

Today's headlines tell us about the voice problems that have been plaguing many of the world's most famous men and women.

Axl Rose of Guns ˗ 'N' Roses was performing on stage in Montreal when his voice gave out. The concert was cut short, and thousands of angered heavy metal fans in the sold-out stadium went on a rampage.

Country singer Kathy Mattea underwent laser surgery on her vocal cords to seal a small blood vessel that had leaked. Larry Gatlin had cysts on his cords, as did Grammy-winning gospel singer Jim Murray. Crystal Gayle, Randy Travis, Ricky Van Shelton, Reba McEntire, Johnny Cash, Michael Jackson and K.T. Oslin have all been under the care of throat specialists. Whitney Houston is reported to have had vocal cord nodules.

In 1995, one of the Presidential hopefuls, Governor Pete Wilson of California, had to delay declaring his candidacy for the White House because he was unable to talk following vocal cord surgery. A few months later when he withdrew from the race he gave as one of the reasons his inability to campaign and raise funds due to his impaired voice.

When Great Britain's Queen Elizabeth appeared

before Parliament recently,   her voice sounded troubled, more subdued than normal, with a rough edge to it. Although Her Highness had a cold at the time, another probable factor was stress. While minor at first, colds, along with stress, can lead to lingering voice problems that, without caution and care, can become serious. It is extremely important to learn how to talk "above" a cold by not letting your voice drop into the lower throat area. Speaking from the lower throat — or deep throat, as I call it — is a no-no, whether you have a cold or not. Deep-throat is spelled T-R-O-U-B-L-E, as I will explain shortly.

A TROUBLED PRESIDENTIAL VOICE: REFLUX, DIET, AND ALLERGY?

The most publicized troubled voice of our times belongs to President Bill Clinton. Throughout the long-winded 1992 Presidential campaign, Clinton battled recurring hoarseness, which forced him to cut short or completely cancel several appearances.

Various medical people consulted by Clinton during the campaign blamed his croaky voice on allergies. Suddenly the energetic Presidential candidate became the nation's number one allergy sufferer. But there was more to Clinton's condition than allergies, said the media. Clinton was also a victim of gastroesophageal reflux, a term for the regurgitation or backflow of corrosive stomach acid being forced up into the esophagus (food pipe). When an overflow of stomach acid reaches into the chest, it causes the fiery sensation commonly known as heartburn. When a small amount bubbles into the throat, it may cause irritation of the vocal cords.

To ease Clinton's condition, the doctors advised him to avoid caffeine, spicy foods, chocolate, and dairy products, because they supposedly thicken laryngeal mucus (vocal cord mucus) and dry up the larynx (voice box), requiring excessive throat-clearing. He was told to drink lots of water and to use a steam inhaler before speaking to "loosen things up."

The words of doctors across the country appeared in magazine and newspaper columns, offering more advice to lessen Clinton's gastroesophageal reflux condition. Do not eat junk food, they warned. Do not sleep on a full stomach. He was cautioned against sleeping on his right side and told to practice silence before speaking.

Meanwhile, the President-to-be continued to take an antihistamine to stave off allergy symptoms. He also received shots to relieve allergy-related irritations.

What do I say to all of this? Pure poppycock!

I do not doubt that President Clinton has allergies and reflux, but in my opinion these conditions are not the primary cause of his voice problems, only ancillary. Millions of us have allergies. Millions have reflux. Many millions of us eat junk food.

WHAT *REALLY* AFFECTS THE PRESIDENT'S VOICE

The doctors are saying those factors discussed above are causing Clinton's hoarseness, and engorging his vocal cords. I am saying that is not really possible since he talks clearly one minute and not the next. No, Clinton's problem cannot basically be attributed to allergies, reflux or junk food. His problem is that he does not know where to direct his voice.

By not knowing where to direct his voice, Clinton is

committing voice suicide. Instead of focusing his voice around the mouth and nose, in the area known as "the mask," he projects from the lower throat around the vocal cords and uses an incorrect pitch range. And that is the fastest route to voice suicide.

Like so many others who have wanted to project an impression of strength and believability, and who have run into severe voice problems along the way, Clinton forces his voice from the lower throat, and the voice box or larynx cannot handle the pressure. Imagine trying to squeeze your feet into shoes that are too small. You may get into the shoes, but you won't walk very far in them.

In my opinion, Bill Clinton may be headed for nodules, polyps, or contact ulcer of the vocal cords or for a very serious condition called "strangled voice" (spasmodic dysphonia). One thing is certain: if he continues to talk hoarsely and have voice trouble, he may lose his voice for variable periods.

I have never met or spoken with the President, but I have considered his public medical records. I have also heard him speak on many public occasions, and I know voices. I don't need a lot of time, only a few seconds, to hear the sound of a healthy voice — or the sound of a voice that is failing.

MISUSED VOICES . . . A NATIONAL PROBLEM

According to my findings, at least twenty-five percent of the people today are experiencing voice problems similar to President Clinton. That is, they are losing their voices by talking from the lower throat.

Another fifty percent talk nasally and too high pitched, which is the worst form of sound pollution.

The nasal voice can turn listeners off, not on, even though we should be accustomed to it. Although such a voice may not tire or become impaired and pathological, listening to it is often difficult, if not impossible. Nasality carries with it too much nasal resonance. Nasal resonance is a key element in keeping a voice well and healthy, allowing it to go on and on, but too much nasal resonance obviously makes you too nasal.

GOOD NASAL RESONANCE VS. NASALITY

Good voices have a marked degree of *nasal* resonance, but not nasality. Richard Crenna and Cheryl Ladd have nasal resonance. They aren't nasal, however. Cyndi Lauper and Sandy Duncan cross the line and have nasality, using too much nasal resonance, as did Howard Cosell. So does the popular Andy Rooney of "60 Minutes."

Woody Allen has a nasal voice, which sounds weak and indecisive. One wonders whether Allen's voice is his own or that of a character he is playing. Can you imagine any of our Presidents delivering a "State of the Union Address" and sounding like Woody Allen? Who would have taken him seriously?

THE DEEP-THROAT VOICE

Deep-throat or lower throat voices sound like those of the living dead. The most notorious of the lower throat talkers is Henry Kissinger. His voice has reached the absolute depths and has become a hypnotizing monotone. Garrison Keillor, whose homespun ramblings are immensely popular, uses a voice on his program that is nearly sleep-inducing. (When speaking before the National Press Club, he spoke in a rich, bass-baritone voice, his real voice.)

These celebrities all have what I call "money voices." I call them that because they are extremely profitable as a calling card and trademark. Their voices make them immediately recognized. The voice quality draws attention to them, defining who they are. These voices are so different and distinctive, they become "money voices" for the individuals using them. They may not have sounds that are appealing to the ear, but they do have *sound recognition*, and they are memorable.

In the coming years, because President Clinton is an authority figure, I anticipate more and more people trying to emulate his sound and talking from the lower throat. As a result, more people than ever before will experience voice problems, only to wind up being treated in many cases by doctors for allergies, reflux, and diet alone, when the problem may be voice misuse and abuse.

GETTING INTO FOCUS — GET THE BUZZ

In all but the rarest of cases, the basic problem with troubled or failing voices is *wrong focus* of the voice, along with incorrect pitch and poor breath support. The proper focus must come from the mask area around the lips and nose.

The voice is built around a "megaphone" extending down from the top of the eyebrows to the bottom of the fifth and sixth cervical vertebrae in the neck, with the narrow portion of the megaphone at the bottom. By dividing the megaphone into thirds, you will find the voice box in the lower one-third. The middle third is the mouth, and the nose is in the upper one-third.

The basic sound of the voice, a very weak sound, comes from the vocal cords located in the larynx (voice box) in the lower portion of the megaphone. The amplification or strengthening of this sound is produced in the mask — around the lips and nose — or as I call it, the "two-thirds solution," referring to the upper two resonance areas of the megaphone.

All good voices are focused in the mask, that is, the two-thirds solution. The blend of oral and nasal resonance, or the buzz, is what creates the vibration in the two-thirds mask area and makes for an efficient and pleasant-sounding voice. This resonance must be blended. (Lower throat resonance is inherent and needs not be stressed.)

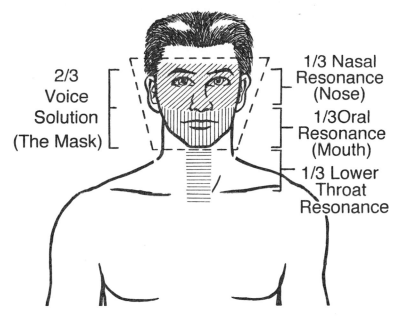

2/3 Voice Solution (The Mask)

1/3 Nasal Resonance (Nose)

1/3 Oral Resonance (Mouth)

1/3 Lower Throat Resonance

Nasal resonance is a key element in making the voice alive and well. As discussed above, too much nasal resonance, however, makes the voice nasal sounding, whiny, and a turn-off. Fear of nasal resonance, or sounding too nasal, causes many people to use lower throat resonance. Forced lower throat resonance leads to voice problems, including a tired weak voice, hoarseness, lack of carrying power, and other negatives associated with a wrong voice.

Mask resonance is the key to a charismatic voice, as well as to voice health and longevity. It provides carrying power, strength and durability of tone. It gives you everything you ever wanted in your voice, and more. Balanced oral and nasal resonance allows you to project your voice easily and comfortably with less or more volume. Good public speakers and talented actors rely on this technique when appearing on stage without the benefit of amplification. What voice fitness is all about is having a voice that works best for you, a voice that is clear, strong and healthy, one that gets you not only heard, but listened to, and liked.

HOW TO FIND YOUR PROPER FOCUS

Getting into voice fitness or voice care is easy. Start by finding the correct focus of your voice with a simple exercise that can automatically place your voice in the mask area, allowing you to hear — and *feel* — your natural voice in seconds.

With your mouth closed, hum the first line of any well-known melody, such as "Happy Birthday." You know how it goes:

Happy birthday to you.
Happy birthday to you.
Happy birthday dear ____.
Happy birthday to you.

This uncomplicated melody should give your real voice a chance to be felt and heard.

A good, healthy voice can come out *naturally*. I stress the word *natural* because this element is essential to finding your true voice. No matter how misused or troubled your voice is now, I find you may be able to almost always talk in a richer, fuller, more *natural* voice — a healthy, sound-good, feel-good voice.

If you didn't hum "Happy Birthday" minutes ago, do it now. Be sure to keep your mouth closed. *Hum*, don't sing. Few people can really sing, but we can all basically hum.

As you hummed, did you hear what happened to your voice? Did you feel it lowering? Or rising? Your voice should move in the direction that is most *natural* for you.

Try gently humming the melody once again. Did you feel a balanced vibration (a buzz) around your nose and lips — in the mask area? You should feel the sound gently reverberating. A good voice is projected from the mask. The vibration helps tell you that your voice is placed correctly.

This simple humming exercise will help you to a better, more effective voice. There will be others as we go along.

Could humming help President Clinton's troubled voice? Indeed, it could. The pitch of his voice is not at fault, it is his *focus*. If he focused his voice correctly, from the mask area rather than from the lower throat, his hoarseness could well disappear. It almost sounds too simple, but it is not. The fact is, he has yet to find his *natural* voice. Ready, Mr. President? Hum "Happy Birthday."

ARE THE PHYSICIANS LISTENING?

In my experience, many doctors, while well-meaning, have not been trained in voice nor to *listen* to voices; therefore, they may not have the understanding necessary to treat patients with troublesome voices, many of whom are seriously inflicted. In medical schools, ear-nose-throat doctors may receive only six hours of instruction in the treatment of voice disorders. Other doctors have basically no training in the speaking voice.

The doctors have only to listen to their patients who return week after week, month after month. They have only to listen to their patients whose voices may continue to go downhill despite debilitating injections, surgeries and medications.

Insofar as diet affecting the voice, the medical researchers have given us much conflicting advice over the years. We were once told that caffeine was bad for us, and that decaffeinated coffee was better. Now, they say, decaf is even more harmful to us than regular coffee.

We have been preached to about the health dangers in eating eggs, only to have that bit of wisdom retracted after tests revealed that eggs are not as evil as they were cracked up to be.

We learned that butter was bad for us, and that margarine was better. Now, we are told, margarine poses more of a health risk than butter.

Will we one day hear that fried foods and meat are actually good for us? Or junk foods, candy and dairy products?

MEDICINE: A WORLD OF EXPERIMENTATION

Sadly, the field of medicine can be a world of experimentation. Medicine gives us many wrong signals that might be misleading. At the end of the nineteenth century, bloodletting was the state of the art medical treatment. Not too long ago, medicine gave us prefrontal lobotomies as state of the art treatment. Perhaps "state of the art treatment" is not the solution.

As discussed in *Change Your Voice, Change Your Life*, Dr. Gershon Lesser, a highly respected internist, was told by three ear-nose-throat specialists that he would not get his voice back without surgery to remove a growth on the vocal fold of his larynx. Dr. Lesser would not give in to surgery; he felt he had other options that were safer and non-invasive. By using my Direct Voice Rehabilitation voice exercises, Dr. Lesser's growth disappeared and he regained a normal, healthy voice.

Dr. Lesser tells me that three-quarters of his patients who consult him for postnasal drip, sinusitis and allergies have voice problems and don't know it.

I find the three conditions of sinusitis, postnasal drip, and allergies, unless they are extreme or pathological, have a minimal, if any effect on the correctly used speaking voice. Unless an infection exists, postnasal drip is a normal condition. Patients make a bugaboo of postnasal drip, believing it is a key factor in their voice problem.

I also received inquires about another condition, deviated septum (partition that divides the nose into two sections). I agree with Friedrich Brodnitz, M.D., who wrote in *Vocal Rehabilitation* (p. 32): "Even pronounced deviations of the septum seem to have little influence on the voice. . . . the indication for a septum operation should be a purely medical one. The operation should not be advised in the hope of improving the voice by a straightening out of the septum."

Medications may give relief and ease emotional and psychological pressures, but they may not deal with the cause of the voice problem — if the cause is voice misuse, mechanically, of the voice itself, including talking in the lower throat, using an incorrect pitch, and/or poor breath support. It is the correct analysis of such voice misuse that eludes those physicians who treat the symptoms of voice misuse basically as being medically related rather than as being caused by poor voice use, a non-medical cause.

MUMBO-JUMBO VOICES

American voices are polluted. They are off-the-wall, nails-on-a-blackboard, achy-breaky voices, bereft of power and listenability. We are in an age of mumbling and mumbo-jumbo. Talk is unintelligible and too often misunderstood. Enunciation may be poor because the voice is poorly used, I find. A voice gone bad may ruin more relationships — personal and professional — than you can imagine.

Here we are with the ultimate, new, state-of-the-art developments in electronics at our fingertips. We are surrounded by sound, in the midst of what has become a sound revolution. These extraordinary marvels of wizardry — voice activated this and sound-sensitive that — are geared to make our lives easier and more pleasurable. But are we ready for them?

Do people understand the messages you leave on their answering machines? Do people ask you to repeat yourself when you talk, either by phone or in person?

What is the condition of your voice? Does your throat feel sore or scratchy following a day or evening of talk? Is your voice rough or gravelly when you speak? Does your voice give out or fade at times? Does it sound weak and troubled? If the answer to any of these questions is "yes," you may be misusing and/or abusing your voice.

IS YOUR OCCUPATION
A THREAT TO YOUR VOICE?

You are especially at risk if speaking is an integral part of your life. I am often asked which occupations are the most threatening to the welfare of the voice. The list is long and varied, but the people at highest risk are those who need to be heard. They are salespeople, lawyers, professors and teachers, the clergy, actors and actresses, singers, politicians, executives, even housewives. They are people who live or work in a stressful, and sometimes noisy, atmosphere. And there are others who work in noisy surroundings where voices must be raised to be heard. In this group are factory workers, musicians, bartenders, aerobic instructors, athletic coaches, among others.

Isn't it time you made your voice work for you, made it strong and listenable — and heard? Can you really afford to lose it?

If your voice is talking to you, and telling you it is in trouble, try helping yourself to a healthy voice through natural voice care. Minor voice problems frequently lead to lingering voice problems, which in turn may become *serious* voice problems.

2

Medicine in Wonderland

In my opinion, President Clinton and his doctors are sending out the wrong message to millions of people. The President and everyone else with voice problems need to get their voices back in gear by properly focusing and balancing the sound in the mask. Voice care is that simple for the President. Pitch change and diaphragmatic breath support may be needed, too.

There are exceptions, of course. When you are ill, say with a cold or the flu, the quality of your voice can be markedly affected, but its efficiency and health needn't be. Yet, I have found that close to twenty percent of all voice problems begin with a cold or upper respiratory condition. That is because the patient with a cold may pamper the voice and misuse it. (The person's voice image contributes to the onset and the change in the mechanical use of his or her voice.) Voice problems stemming from a cold or the flu should not be ignored. Keep your pitch focused in the mask and see if it helps you. Lozenges, gargles or sprays may help your voice improve, but they are really not cure-alls. In my experience, they may provide only temporary symptomatic relief.

TIPS FOR AILING VOICES

Your voice is a *sturdy* instrument, not delicate as is generally believed. If used properly your voice will hold up under almost all circumstances and be a valuable physical asset. You must, however, take care when illness strikes. When you become fatigued, it is too easy to "baby" the voice by letting it do what it wants to do in your weakened condition. This is wrong. Watch your pitch and focus. Be careful that you don't let your voice drop so you are talking from the lower throat. The husky sound of laryngitis may impress your boss if you call in sick, and you may even sound sexy, but you need not head for disaster.

One more tip: Avoid *excessive* amounts of irritants, such as alcohol and tobacco. It is only common sense to limit your intake, especially if you are not feeling up to par. Moderate alcohol intake may be relaxing; excessive alcohol on a continual basis may contribute to an inefficient use of the speaking voice. A voice that is right may soon go wrong with too much alcohol. You become so relaxed that your voice drops down into your lower throat, the danger zone.

Smoking can have an irritating effect on the vocal cords and on the lungs. Unfortunately, smoking is sometimes used to achieve a husky or deepened voice. If that is your aim, you don't have to smoke. A deeper, fuller voice can be yours with voice help.

VOICE SUICIDE: MISUSE VS. ABUSE

Throughout the pages of this book I emphasize the words *misuse* and *abuse* as factors leading to problem voices. It is important, however, to understand the specific differences between them so you may avoid both misusing and abusing your voice.

Voice *misuse* means using the wrong voice in pitch (too high or too low), in tone focus (too nasal or too deep-throat), in quality (hoarseness, breathiness, nasality), in volume (too loud or too soft), in breath support (too much movement from the shoulders or upper chest as well as reverse breathing or inadequate breath support), and in rate (too fast or too slow).

Voice *abuse* involves excessive shouting, screaming, yelling, or even loud talking over a period of time. That may happen from cheering on your favorite team, from constant talking to someone who is hard of hearing, or from talking over or under the sound of air conditioning, television, machinery, and traffic noise.

Avoid voice misuse and abuse if you can, particularly if you are in one of the more susceptible professions that requires effective speaking, as I mentioned earlier. Actually, almost everyone should be included, because eighty percent of all communication is carried out through the spoken word. If your voice is troubled, and you want to speak up or out, it may be difficult to be heard or understood. Your voice then becomes a distraction. More importantly, it may affect your health and your well-being.

Millions of Americans are misusing their voices, playing a disastrous voice game I call voice *suicide*. Basically, voice suicide is the conscious or unconscious damage an individual inflicts upon his or her voice. It results from long-term voice misuse and/or abuse and can lead to very serious voice damage. Most of us have suffered temporary voice failure because of strain or laryngitis, which makes the simplest daily talking activities become difficult, if not impossible. Even routine functions like answering the phone or greeting a friend become major challenges. The fortunate ones get their voices back. For too many others, however, the condition lingers and worsens.

Voice misuse and/or abuse can lead to a tired or fatigued voice, which may be the beginning of organic voice problems, such as vocal cord growths (nodes, polyps, or contact ulcers of the vocal cords). For others, their voices take on either a strained, strangled or choked sound, often with constant short breaks, or they become choppy and breathy, whispery, with an irregular voice tremor at times. You may get a strangled voice or a condition medically called spasmodic dysphonia or spastic dysphonia, also referred to as SD. (Spasmodic dysphonia is the more common; it is intermittent. Spastic dysphonia is less common; the voice basically remains strangled throughout communication.)

There are two types of spasmodic dysphonia or spastic dysphonia. The more prevalent is called *ad*ductor spasmodic dysphonia (vocal cords too tight). Less common is *ab*ductor spasmodic dysphonia (vocal cords too open). An acronym for the two types of strangled voice, which defines the condition, is "SAD." In normal voice, vocal cords approximate.

THE DARK SOUNDS OF THE
STRANGLED VOICE OR SD

Spasmodic dysphonia or SD isn't only strangled and whispered sounds. Victims of SD may also have choked voices, missed or breaking speech sounds, missed voicing (silence), effortful or squeezed tone, jerky staccato sound, voice stoppage, excessive pressure, or a hostile sounding quality.

Want to hear the sound of SD? Try this experiment. First, exhale completely so that your lungs are totally free of air. Now, without breathing in, count slowly to 50 out loud. You may not need to count that high to get the idea.

First identified in 1871, SD has been around for a long time. In the absence of any visible pathology — inflamed throat, vocal cord polyps or nodules — the patients may be misdiagnosed and, therefore, mistreated. Unfortunately, once the condition is diagnosed, the patients are also told that it is hopeless and permanent, that there is no known cure, no recovery. The American Speech-Language-Hearing Association in its journal, *Asha*, in November 1993 explicitly said that no cure for spasmodic dysphonia exists at the present time. (p. 65)

Wrong, wrong, *wrong.*

Forget what you have heard or read. In fact, hopeless may not be hopeless at all. To the doctors, SD is a mystery. To me, it is the mystery that isn't.

HOPE FOR HOPELESS VOICES

My successes with SD run contrary to the doomsayers in the world of medicine and, sadly, are unacceptable to medicine and speech pathology. Perhaps that is because my successes were achieved without resorting to the revered but manqué practices of "the establishment." These patients, many of whom were long-suffering, including some who were surgically treated or provided with botulinum toxin, were helped through a completely safe, non-toxic method called Direct Voice Rehabilitation.

Now meet Gayle. Gayle *had* spastic dysphonia.

Gayle worked in sales, so she has to talk a lot throughout the day. Her voice was vital to her in leading a normal productive life.

Her voice problem started as so many others do, with a cold. She talked in the lower throat, and her voice began to deteriorate. Soon her body reacted in sympathy. Hardly a morning passed that she wanted to get out of bed.

Gayle saw a doctor who listened to her chest. "He told me it sounded like I was a heavy, heavy smoker," she says, "and I don't smoke at all." She was given a series of antibiotics, each one stronger than the last. "The medications made me feel better, but they didn't help my voice."

Gayle was losing her voice. As she continued to force herself to talk, misusing her voice by speaking from the lower throat, her throat grew sore. "My voice was scratchy and raspy," she says. "It hurt to talk."

Seeking relief, Gayle went from doctor to doctor. During a six-month period she visited nine different doctors and speech clinicians. Her vocal cords were injected with a muscle relaxant. Her voice became clear, but only for less than two hours. As the medication wore off, her troubled voice returned.

One clinician had her doing exercises, making different sounds using "E" words and "H" words. Her voice went in and out, mostly out. She was diagnosed at UCLA Medical Center's Head and Neck Division as having both adductor *and* abductor spastic dysphonia. Her options were either surgery or injection into the vocal cords of botulinum toxin, more commonly known as Botox.

THE BOTOX STORY

Until a few years back, cutting into the recurrent laryngeal nerve, which paralyzes a healthy vocal cord, was all the rage. Today's rage is injections of Botox.

Botox is a sugar-coated, glorified Madison Avenue term, but like "a rose by any other name . . .," it is still a deadly poison used in attenuated form. In 1989, the Federal Drug Administration stated that treatment using botulin "was no longer experimental but an established medical practice" — but "for only two . . . diseases, blepharospasm and adult strabismus." (*Discover*, p. 32) Spasmodic dysphonia was not included. However, the medical profession, I hear and read, basically swears by Botox and injects doses into the vocal cords of patients with SD.

Here are some facts about the Botox poison, which should be of interest to you, as described in *Discover* (August 1992), pp. 29-33 and *Our Voice* (Fall 1992), p. 4:

• It is produced by two biochemists, 84-year-old Ed Schantz, who perfected its development, and 36-year-old Eric Johnson.

• "When ingested, botulin causes botulism, a form of food poisoning that can result in muscle paralysis and even death." (p. 30) (Johnson has noted that "botulin is six *million* times more toxic than rattlesnake venom," which, for reasons of employee safety, has caused most drug companies to back away.) It is said to be effective in small doses as a treatment for dystonias — uncontrollable muscle spasms that researchers suspect are caused by involuntary, excessive impulses from the brain.

• The toxin works "by attaching itself to nerve endings." (p. 30) People who die of botulism generally suffocate, because their chest muscles have become paralyzed.

• In the making of botulin for clinical use, the delicate procedures are as much "touch and lore" as technical knowledge. Admits Schantz: "A lot of these things (steps) are judgment calls." (p. 33)

• The toxin is so powerful that Schantz and Johnson are still working from a crop of bacteria produced in 1979. This batch was acquired in 1990 by Allergan Pharmaceuticals. According to Johnson, Allergan "just walked into it . . . without having to invest the years of development and high research costs that accompany most drug research." (p. 33)

POISONED VOCAL CORDS . . .

On one hand doctors tell SD patients their condition is hopeless. On the other hand they say that medical procedures will help them get symptom relief if they have SD. The use of surgery or Botox has not reported one single cure that I know of. Surgery indicates success as a breathy voice, often a temporary relief of the spasticity. Botox may be repeated every one to three to six months, and I find the result is often not a clear voice. The voice comes and goes for most patients. They need repeated doses and nobody knows the long-term, downside effects of this substance on the body.

At a leading medical center, one of my SD patients, who had been Botoxed a number of times and still couldn't talk, was told by her ear-nose-throat doctor that Botox was the state of the art treatment and was 99% effective. Another patient of mine, who had been Botoxed forty times, still did not have a voice. A third patient who was Botoxed over a dozen times also did not have a voice.

"If we can't cure you at least we'll awe you with
modern medical technology."

From *The Wall Street Journal* - Permission, Cartoon Features Syndicate

A SAFE, ALTERNATIVE APPROACH

Patients that I have seen, who have been Botoxed, may look to Direct Voice Rehabilitation as the alternative non-medical approach. People with SD are calling me from all over the United States, Canada, Europe, and South America, as well as coming in for treatment.

Recently, a patient told me that she had received a call from a prestigious clinic (where she had gone for an evaluation), telling her that in thirty minutes they were doing the Botox shots and would fit her in. She was so upset by the directive of "Hurry in to get your Botox shot," that she came to see me the following week.

In my view, medicine in this regard is like the emperor in his new clothing: Naked. As I see it, basically doctors do not understand how to treat the functional voice problem, which includes SD.

Incidentally, Botox is now being used at Columbia

Presbyterian Hospital in New York City for the elimination of facial wrinkles, according to *Cosmopolitan* (October 1993, p. 66). However, as with Botox injections in the vocal cords, the effects of the "face lift" may last only four to six months.

Gayle would not commit to any treatment until she did her research.

Gayle didn't like what she discovered about the surgical process for SD. ("Very little can be said about surgery that is good," she comments.) She also refused to have poison shot into her body. Feeling that her situation was indeed hopeless, she became "very different, very withdrawn, very unhappy. And I am usually a very outgoing person." At that point, when Gayle was at her lowest, Dr. Gerald Berke, head of UCLA's Head and Neck Division, referred Gayle to me after she had requested a non-toxic, non-surgical approach.

Says Gayle: "With Dr. Cooper I went from a 'hopeless' spastic dysphonic voice to a clear voice in about ten seconds. He brought my voice back *that* quickly, in one session. That first day it went in and out a little, but by the third session I had my voice back completely."

Initially, Gayle experienced "morning voice" for a time. Morning voice is something most everyone has when they first awaken and the voice is low pitched and guttural.

"I can deal with that," says Gayle, "because I can talk again. My voice is clear throughout the day, and it doesn't hurt. My old scratchy, raspy voice did hurt."

FROM STRANGLED SOUNDS (SD)
TO A NORMAL VOICE

Following Gayle's visits to my office, she was referred back to the UCLA Medical Center for a phonatory workup. This was done to compare her new voice to her old spastic dysphonic voice, and she was found to have a normal voice. Her recovery had taken only three sessions. However, Gayle had no voice image to speak of, and she had the ear, the willingness, and the ability to get her voice back quickly. She is unusual. Most SD patients need extensive Direct Voice Rehabilitation.

Gayle's voice remains excellent four years after completing a program of Direct Voice Rehabilitation.

A DIFFERENT VOICE IMAGE

A major factor in changing from a wrong, troubled voice to a right, healthy voice is your voice image. The voice image is the way you hear yourself. It influences you psychologically and emotionally to remain with the old voice as you find and use your new natural voice. Your old voice had become part of you, and you had grown so accustomed to it that any alteration may make you uncomfortable for a time. The new voice may sound too loud, too full, too rich, and too different. If you ask others about your new voice, they will almost always tell you it sounds extremely credible and natural. You must discard your old voice image and establish, as well as accept, a new voice image based on your new, natural voice.

Most people comment about their new voice sounding "different." At first it will sound and feel unnatural. But don't be discouraged. Soon your voice can begin to feel both natural and normal.

PRESSING YOUR MAGIC BUTTON

How did Gayle regain her natural voice so quickly? She began by using my "Instant Voice Press," an exercise that has been so successful that patients often refer to it as "pressing your magic button."

The Instant Voice Press is a holistic technique that basically gives you the correct tone focus, natural pitch level and range, and the sound of your real voice. The Instant Voice Press is a simple 3-for-1 procedure that may give you everything "in a nutshell." (NOTE: If there are any medical problems involving the area of the solar plexus or the abdomen, or if you are pregnant, DO NOT attempt this exercise.)

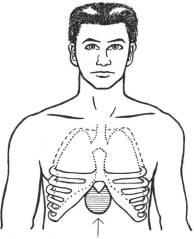

Bottom of Breast Bone (Solar Plexus)

The
Cooper Instant
Voice Press

To use my Instant Voice Press, begin by placing one hand on your solar plexus, the center area at the bottom of your breast bone (or between the solar plexus and the navel). Now relax your stomach so that it moves in and out as you breathe. With your lips closed, hum while repeatedly pressing your solar plexus gently with your fingers in a light, quick rhythm "Hmmmmmm." (Hold that *h m m m m m m*.) "Hmmmmm." "Hmmmmm." This gentle jiggling of the solar plexus will cause your "hmmmm" to break up into short bursts of sound like "hmmm-hmmm-hmmm-hmmm-hmmm . . ."

Do this exercise once again. Close your lips and hum while lightly pressing your fingers, gently jiggling, at the bottom of the breast bone where the two sides of the rib cage join. As the sound escapes, you will feel a buzz around your mouth and nose. You are actually directing your voice into the mask area, precisely where it should be.

Next, do the Instant Voice Press with your mouth open, saying "Ahhhhhhh."

Try the exercise again, this time adding a number as you press. Start with "hmm-hmm-one," "hmm-hmm-two," "hmm-hmm-three." Then use "ahh-ahh-one," "ahh-ahh-two," "ahh-ahh-three."

Finally, carry this sound over to talking, beginning with one word at a time. "Ahh-my-ahh-name-ahh-is-ahh ___." Keep the sentence short and learn to talk on the buzz, which is a resonance around the lips and nose.

Can you achieve that same focus and pitch level without pressing your magic button? Raise both hands high above your head and repeat the following words with energy. "RIGHT." "NO." "REALLY." I call these words "buzz words" because they help bring your real voice forward.

Whenever you seem unable to locate your correct pitch level and focus, revert to the Instant Voice Press and use the "hmmm," "ahhh," and buzz words. I have used these techniques for years to help individuals find their real voices in seconds. It is a good idea to start your day with these exercises. (In the movie, *Sister Act*, I noticed that Sister Mary Clarence, played by Whoopi Goldberg, used the Instant Voice Press on another Sister to bring her efficient singing voice out.)

THE SILENT REVEREND

The Reverend Harold's voice problem was equally severe, but Harold had suffered with a troubled voice for twelve years. For two of those years he could barely speak at all.

When Harold first visited a doctor, he was given a series of tests. He was then treated for an upper respiratory infection. At one point Harold was told by his doctor that he was deaf in one ear. The ear was operated on, but Harold still had a voice problem.

Harold next made an appointment at the University of California at Irvine, where a woman he knew with a similar voice problem was being treated. At UCI, he was tested again. The doctors there were hesitant in their prognosis, not being sure if Harold actually had SD; but they recommended he be injected with Botox poison anyway. He was told that the shot would give him relief even though his voice would get raspy.

Botox poison was injected into both of Harold's vocal cords. He did get some relief, but he lost his voice. Three days later Harold was forcing a whisper as he presided at a funeral.

The injection effect continued over a nine-month period. Says Harold, "I never had a clear voice during that time. To the contrary, it was always raspy, very breathy, and speaking was difficult at times. The doctors never really talked to me, except to tell me there was no cure for my condition. Every so often I was sent reminders to come in for the next shot. By the way, those shots are not cheap."

Looking back, Harold believes that the botulinum toxin contributed to the continuing decline of his voice. "I should never have taken the poison," he says. "It was a very poor first option."

His voice growing worse, Harold changed doctors and new tests were given. At UCLA he was told, as he reported to me, that he had developed spasmodic dysphonia "because of increased pressure on his voice." Injections of Botox poison were recommended. Harold declined.

With Harold's voice continuing its downhill slide, he began to learn more about spasmodic dysphonia, including the fact that he was not alone in his suffering. Spasmodic dysphonia, Harold found, seemed to be common among ministers, teachers, and others who use their voices in a prolonged way. He felt if he could find the right voice coach, someone who could place his voice correctly, he might be all right.

INDIRECT VS. DIRECT APPROACH

Harold spent six months with a speech clinician, Dr. Z., who had him doing neck exercises to stretch the muscles in his throat. "Your throat muscles have tightened up over the years," Dr. Z. told him.

Harold was told to take warm showers, letting the

water run down and along his throat to relax the muscles. "Stretch your neck from side to side with your mouth wide open," was more advice. Harold did the exercises unfailingly. They had no effect at all on his voice.

A vocal exercise came next. Harold began climbing the musical scale with his voice, going from a low pitch to a high pitch. Low to high, high to low, over and over again. That didn't help either.

(The neck stretches, warm showers and scale climbing are among the exercises used by speech clinicians. This I term the *indirect approach*. The classic training taught at Stanford University, where I studied voice training, was the *direct approach*, which I refined using natural, simple techniques. This evolved into Direct Voice Rehabilitation or DVR which is basically unknown in this country, I find.)

Surgery became another option for Harold. Again, he declined. He knew that once he had gone under the surgeon's knife his condition could never be reversed.

It was Harold's ENT (ear/nose/throat doctor), Dr. Gerald Berke, who referred Harold to me after Harold requested a non-invasive approach.

THE DANGER ZONE

Like every SD patient who has come to my office, Harold was speaking from his lower throat, which I call the "danger zone." SD patients *always* speak from the lower throat. In over twenty years of successfully treating SD, I have never found an exception. Medicine and I agree that the SD voice is in the lower throat. But here's where we disagree.

Medicine calls it "a focal laryngeal dystonia." That

means it is a neurological problem and therefore, treated medically. I find SD not a dystonia, but a *dysphonia*, from mechanical use of the wrong voice unknowingly, or voice misuse and abuse.

Not only was Harold speaking from the lower throat, his pitch was incorrect and he did not use diaphragmatic breathing. We have all been told as children to stand up straight, with "chest out, stomach in!" We never really learned *why*, of course, but the reasoning behind the almost constant reminders was that good posture increased air to the lungs, which, in turn, exercised and expanded our chest muscles, making our blood richer and better.

Unfortunately, that advice was all wrong. Have you ever noticed how a baby's abdomen rises and falls with each breath? Babies breathe as nature intended, from the midsection, without any instruction at all. When you breathe properly, using your midsection (stomach muscles), you relieve tension in the muscles of the lower throat and increase oxygen intake, allowing your voice to project more easily. As your stomach pumps the air up through your mouth and nose, the air reinforces the voice to make it richer, fuller, more resonant, and durable. We cannot talk well without supported, controlled air.

MIDSECTION OR DIAPHRAGMATIC BREATHING

For those who have heard the expression, "Speak from the diaphragm," let me explain the real meaning of the term and its significance. Diaphragmatic breathing is a popular term which means belly breathing, stomach breathing, central breathing, or midsection breathing (or breath support). The diaphragm is a muscle of inhalation which separates the chest cavity from the stomach. Four sets of paired muscles, the rectus abdominus, the transverse abdominus, and the external and internal oblique abdominus, control exhalation; these are a corset of muscles covering the stomach. They are already in place, waiting to be used, if you simply use them properly for breath support. You needn't work out to get them in shape. The expression "Speak from the diaphragm" is a misnomer; we speak from the stomach muscles that control air flowing through the vocal cords for speaking or singing. Few people ever use midsection breath support for speaking; singers use it for singing, but basically not for speaking. People who have SD are notoriously lacking in midsection breath support.

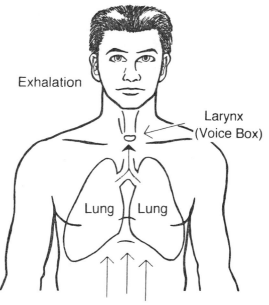

(Stomach) Pushes Air Out

TALKING WITHOUT AIR

People who have voice problems, especially severe voice problems such as "the strangled voice" or SD, often reverse the breathing process. They push the stomach out as they talk, instead of letting the stomach move in. (One approach I do not understand is reverse breathing, or what is referred to as "donkey breathing" *purposely* being taught to SD patients. Perhaps I am missing something.) Other patients let the air out before they talk or as they start to talk. Still others run out of air as they speak. Rather than stopping to take a breath, they keep on talking, waiting until the end of the sentence to breathe. By holding their breath, letting the air out, or reversing the breathing process, they are actually speaking without air — or with only a minimal amount of reserve air. You cannot drive a car on empty. Nor can you speak on empty, without air. (I am reminded of one particular patient, a young lady with SD, who made the following startling comment when I noted she didn't breathe when she spoke: "I'll talk now," she said, "and breathe later.")

The average person breathes eight to twelve times per minute, more if under stress. The chest cavity is heavy and requires considerable energy to lift up and out. Expanding the chest with every breath is not only pointless, it is exhausting.

The Reverend Harold was not supporting his voice; he was keeping his stomach out without letting it move in as he talked. I explained the proper breathing technique to him, then had him try to talk — using midsection breath support — saying "um-hmmm" instead of words, as if he were responding to someone in conversation.

"Say 'um-hmm'," I asked of Harold. "Keep your lips

together and try not to force the sound. Be as spontaneous and sincere as possible."

"Um-hmmm," Harold replied.

"Again."

"Um-hmmm. Um-hmmm."

"Now say 'um-hmm' once more, and follow it with the number 'one'. Say 'um-hmm . . . one'."

"Um-hmm . . . one."

As Harold did the exercise I heard a noticeable difference in his voice. The "um-hmm" brought out his natural voice, but he reverted to his damaged voice when saying the word "one." I had him try again, keeping the "um-hmm" and "one" at the same pitch level and tone focus.

"Um-hmm . . . one. Um-hmm . . . one."

Once Harold had his voice focused in the mask, away from the lower throat, I had him lower his pitch level. He practiced using "buzz words," such as "Right," then "Right now," and finally talking on that sound. His voice was full and resonant.

By the end of our session on that first day, Harold's voice was almost back to normal. He had found his natural voice very quickly and easily. Keeping it was another matter. By speaking incorrectly for so many years, Harold had built up bad voice habits. Without concentrating on the proper speaking techniques, it is easy to slide back into the old ways. Add vocational pressures, stress, daily interfacing with people and speaking engagements, and the cycle could start over again. However, today you would never know he once had a very serious voice problem, when he attends to his voice. When he doesn't, his spasticity is still there. It is up to Harold to self-monitor himself and keep aware of what is essential for him to speak easily and correctly until it becomes habitual. I stress that you must attend to your voice. You, like Harold, control your voice destiny.

"POISON IS A POOR CHOICE"

Says Harold: "I feel that a person with SD has only one option — voice therapy. Poison is a poor choice. It doesn't bring back your old voice, not even close. It does relax the vocal cords some but it also creates some difficulties. My personal doctor really opposed the procedure. She advised me not to take the injections because botulinum poison is one of the most toxic poisons known to man. Her concern was the poison getting into my system. The doctors who administered Botox didn't say if it was safe or not. They never mentioned the possible long-term downside effects of the poison, never made me aware. I assumed Botox was safe because the doctors were using it."

Harold adds, "I have trouble understanding why the medical field would want to give toxin as a first option when voice therapy is not invasive. If voice therapy didn't work, then try toxin. But *direct* voice therapy does work, and it doesn't do a number on you like toxin does."

SEEK OPTIONS . . . NOT THE EASY CURE

In defense of the medical establishment, I must say that its use of botulinum toxin is an earnest attempt at helping vocally disabled patients with SD. However, I strongly disagree with the field in general, as well as with many of my colleagues in speech pathology. Patients today seek the easy cure, whether by pills,

injections, or the quick cut. For the SD patient —
typically despairing and depressed by their
"inexplicable" loss of voice — medicine advises the
magic of a shot or surgery. To me, that is wrong. The
patient should first be given the option of direct voice
therapy, a procedure that is non-invasive, safe, and
with no downside effects.

Recently, *The Crusaders,* a popular investigative
television series presented a segment entitled "Endless
Silence." This show described my approach to SD and
how I treat it by a non-medical natural way, with
recoveries covering twenty years, which indicates there
is another way to help patients with so-called hopeless
voices. It isn't the only way. My way takes time and
effort and involves the cooperation of the patient. My
way requires you change the way you use your voice,
and it requires you to become part of the doctoring that
is needed to bring the voice back to efficiency and
health. My way is not for everyone when it comes to
the strangled voice. My approach to SD is an option
and an alternative to surgery, which was once the rage,
and Botox, which is now the rage.

The Crusaders' segment brought me calls from
people some of whom told me they had been Botoxed,
could not talk, and did not want to continue Botox
because of concern with the long range effect on the
body and the voice. A lady from Florida called me in
panic after having received Botox shots for two years.
As I was struggling to hear her still broken voice, she
said, "But I haven't had a heart attack." A heart attack?
Is that the chance a patient must take to be able to
speak normally again?

One individual reported curling of her lips and
tongue after having taken Botox treatments. Could
curling be another possible side effect of the poison?

Her doctor believes that curling stems from dyspraxia, a neurological disability, not the Botox. What are the negative effects of Botox? I wonder.

Another person who called told of a severe reaction from a Botox injection. When she called her physician at a leading medical center, at first she was told the reaction was normal and she was imagining the problem. Later the center affirmed that she had received an injection from a "bad batch," and that other patients had been affected.

I also received calls from individuals who told me they had been Botoxed for benign growths on the vocal cords when surgery did not work or when speech therapy was not doing the job. I had not known that Botox was being used for such routine benign growths of the vocal cords, but I did learn that from some callers.

FREEING THE PATIENT FROM MEDICAL DEPENDENCY

I find it interesting that some doctors appear to seek medical intervention by Botox to treat nodules, polyps, and contact ulcers — problems that the medical field in past years has acknowledged to be in the province and jurisdiction of speech pathology. I differ with the current orientation of what I am hearing about the ever widening medical use of Botox for benign growths, because it seems to me to create a voice that isn't natural in use but dependent upon medical supervision and control, possibly making the patient rely on ongoing medical intervention for voice care and help. My approach seeks to free the patient from dependency upon anyone except the patient.

Botox poison is not a cure-all, not even a cure. The fact is, to my knowledge there are no known cures with Botox, and the improvement factor, I find, is more often than not minimal and temporary with the voice. The injections I am told may be painful, expensive, and repeated at regular intervals. The poison is believed to be safe in the short-term, but the long-term effects are unknown. "Short-term" and "long-term" are relative. The possibility of severe side effects in ten years may mean different things to a twenty-six year old and a seventy year old. In either case, the patient should be advised of potential risks.

Surgery does not seek to produce a normal voice. If it is successful in relieving spasticity (the strangled sound), it essentially leaves the patient with a breathy, whispery voice all too often. And that is too often the norm of success for surgery.

All voice pathologists are not the same; in the hands of a competent direct voice clinician, voice therapy can do no harm. It seeks a normal voice. A normal, healthy voice.

Doctors are trained to do medical procedures. But they have also taken an oath to *do no harm*. It is a wonderful creed, and should be closely adhered to in all aspects of healing.

To condemn the medical field in general would be a gross injustice. All I am saying is, if you have a voice problem and the help you are getting from your doctor works for you and has a lasting effect, fine. If it isn't working, don't give up. Try another approach to heal your voice — a safer, easier, more positive way to a healthy voice.

Ask questions of your doctor, and don't take everything he or she says as gospel. Remember, you <u>do</u> have choices. Know your options by insisting that your doctor tell you about them. As Norman Cousins said, during a lecture at UCLA (September 26, 1985), the job of the physician is to provide to the patient the latest and best available from medical science.

There is hope for "hopeless" voices, just as there is hope for most everything in life if only you find the right person — and the right approach.

3

De-Mystify and De-Medicalize

Perhaps it is appropriate at this time to de-mystify and de-medicalize as well as de-glamourize voice care. Perhaps it is time to empower voice patients to secure informed consent about options and alternatives to medical intervention. Some doctors may be misleading their patients by seeing a one-sided picture of the voice problem. By not having a larger view or understanding of not only the functional or non-organic voice problem itself, but also how to deal with it nonsurgically, some medical doctors don't know what to do — and that includes some of the big names, the so-called hierarchy. But many of these doctors have had no real training in voice. When the problem is not organic, they often prescribe medications. These doctors may be actually contributing to the medicating of America.

This point was brought home clearly by one of my patients, Jim, an executive in the banking field. His problem started in late 1988. Jim had left his hometown for New York City to take a job that kept him on the phone from eight to ten hours a day. It was a high pressure job and he soon developed chronic, recurrent laryngitis by day's end. As his voice grew weaker, his throat and neck areas became very painful by the end of the work day.

As Jim remembers, he saw four or five doctors and two speech therapists, including Dr. X., a leading ENT doctor, who concluded that Jim's problem was not organic. "When Dr. X. said to me, 'You're straining it somehow,' without any further explanation, that was it. I walked out, past all the celebrity photos on his walls; I was aware that Dr. X. was the doctor of famous celebrities, a 'top banana'."

At two hospitals, Mt. Sinai and Manhattan Ear and Eye, Jim was given pills, pills and more pills to control allergies and saliva. Unable to find relief in New York from the doctors, therapists or pills, he quit his job, went on disability, and moved back to his home town to be near his fiancee. Home again, he found a less demanding job, one that he felt put fewer strains on his voice. But his voice did not improve with the changes, and the soreness in his throat did not go away. He was becoming increasingly anxious and depressed.

FROM DOCTOR TO DOCTOR . . . TO DOCTOR

Jim next visited the office of Dr. Y., where an esophageal wrap procedure was among the potential procedures that was discussed, though only as a last resort. Jim's condition was diagnosed as dysphonia and acid reflux. (The laryngological medical literature increasingly look to reflux [GERD or Gastroesophageal Reflux Disease] as the likely source of chronic laryngitis and hoarseness, with voice misuse usually not given appropriate or adequate attention.) Jim was given a number of acid reflux medicines and accompanying speech therapy to no avail. "I ran through money very quickly taking tranquilizers, pain pills and anti-reflux medications," he says. Throughout most of 1989 Jim stayed on that program without improvement, although Dr. Y. insisted Jim was "getting better."

Another 15 doctors, masseurs, acupuncturists, and psychiatrists followed. Dr. Y.'s thesis was that Jim's condition was improving. It wasn't. "They had me doing speech therapy, which turned out to be very Rube Goldberg. I was told to hold my tongue flat when I talk, or curl it to the back of my teeth. I was told I had tremendous jaw tension. Dr. Y.'s clinician told me to run my consonants together. To do that I had to contract my throat enough to create audible friction, which put even more strain on my aching throat muscles. A psychiatrist told me that I hated my grandmother. My feelings toward her, he said, made me cynical, and that was causing me to lose my voice. I couldn't believe that one!"

READY TO GIVE UP

Although not a quitter by nature, Jim began to think no one could help him. He had spent over $30,000 on what he now calls "shrinks, speech therapists, masseurs, tea leaf readers and total wildness." Yet his voice remained rough and croaky, and the pain in his throat was at times intolerable. "I'd go on Advil binges to suppress the pain and swelling," he says. "I became an Advil junkie." At one point he was so mentally and physically down that he became borderline suicidal.

Fortunately, through it all, however, Jim did not give up. He remembers sitting in Dr. Y.'s outer office during the summer of 1990, talking to a fellow patient (who had SD) he had come to know. With effort, they began to exchange thoughts and compare notes.

During their time together, Jim's friend mentioned a book by Dr. Cooper, *Change Your Voice, Change Your Life* and asked if he had read it. "I hadn't," says Jim, "but I got a copy and read it over the weekend." Jim recognized his plight through the stories related in the book and was on a plane to L.A. very shortly.

Jim visited me in L.A. in August of 1990. "I saw a 50% improvement in my voice within three days. But I wanted more. With Dr. Cooper in California, I began searching for a doctor in my area who used his method of Direct Voice Rehabilitation. That became a problem. There was nobody. In my search, however, I met a patient who had had a paralyzed vocal cord and had been told his career was over. He had gotten his voice back with Dr. Cooper. I worked with that gentleman between semi-annual trips to L.A.

"Dr. Cooper originally diagnosed my problem, myasthenia laryngis, in half an hour. Originally I was talking too low. Then, in doing the exercises on my own and with a fellow patient, I went too high to compensate for the wrong focus. To counteract that, I went too low again. Now, with Dr. Cooper's help, I'm in the right pitch. I've had no problems at all since Christmas, 1992, and I'm doing more talking than ever. My voice has become a tool rather than a liability, and I now have regular public speaking engagements in addition to my job-related telephone work."

"IT'S A NUTHOUSE OUT THERE . . ."

While Jim is thrilled to be speaking clearly again, and without pain, he is angry about the negative experiences he encountered in his search to find a cure for his voice problem. "It is a nuthouse out there," he says. "Most of the doctors and therapists I encountered were of little help, and that includes some well-known East Coast doctors who have a hammerlock on the field. They seem to be almost Mephistophelean gurus of voice. They control what is said and what is done, what we hear and what we read. They never referred me to Dr. Cooper when their methods weren't working. How that's possible, I don't know.

"On second thought, maybe I do. It seems to come down to the influence wielded by certain doctors.

"When Bill Clinton came on the scene, reflux became the hot topic. Also, one of the first questions you're asked when you enter doctors' offices is, 'What's your insurance number?' And you know what? Reflux is a reimbursable condition. I think that's why it is now the rage. The insurance companies will pay for treatment. In other words, any billable procedure is okay. If it isn't billable, you don't have it. In fact, one doctor told me that there was 'no code' for Dr. Cooper's diagnosis, so I couldn't have it!"

A VOICE MYSTERY

Everybody loves a good mystery, but not in a doctor's office. Is there any field of medicine as baffling, contradictory, or mystifying as voice rehabilitation? I have seen patients who have been bamboozled into accepting voice treatments that were outdated, expensive and ineffectual. The overwhelming number of patients I have seen do not require an MRI, CAT scan, extensive research, and extensive testing with an extensive team approach.

My team approach is in stark contrast to the medical approach. My team involves the clinician's ear, a cooperative patient, a knowledgeable ENT doctor, and assistance from a spouse or a friend in severe cases. Additionally, I use a unique method of having consenting patients communicate with and help each other in group situations or one-on-one. My team approach is simple, but it works wonders.

THE PROFIT GAME

The government is concerned over the high costs of health care for the American public. It isn't only the high costs. It's the needless spending, the waste and excesses, the lining of pockets at the expense of the government — and the unsuspecting public. Has profit become the name of the game?   Are the doctors complaining?   The drug companies?   The manufacturers of medical equipment and supplies?

Good voice health doesn't have to cost that much. There are alternate ways — safer, more effective, less costly treatments and remedies that may not be offered to you.

I am reminded of a line in the movie of Robin Cook's bestselling novel, *Coma.* Speaking of patients, the Chief of Surgery says: "They're like children. They trust us."

We are all much too trusting today, especially when it comes to illness of any kind. We want the quick fix, the "faster the better" cure. Cut if off, cut it out, inject it, medicate it, whatever — just get rid of it. Don't be in such a rush. Chances are, there are better ways to help you to a happy, healthier voice life.

BAND-AID TREATMENTS

Although little is heard about it publicly, palliative treatment is very much in vogue today. Do you know the meaning of *palliate* ? The dictionary says: (1) To cloak; shelter; hide. (2) To mitigate; to ease without curing; as to *palliate* a disease. (3) To cover with excuses; to extenuate; as to *palliate* faults.

As early as 20 years ago, in a textbook I authored, *Modern Techniques of Vocal Rehabilitation,* I included a section on palliative treatment. Here are some thoughts on the subject from that book:

"Most functional dysphonic patients are afforded palliative measures to deal with their voice problems. Frequently patients have been given antibiotics (injections and medication) for many months in order to resolve a voice disorder. This method of treatment is utilized by a number of laryngologists who remain unaware that the inflammation of the vocal folds may be due to misuse of voice rather than to viruses, allergies, and infections.

"Tarneaud, a well-known laryngologist, wrote in 1958:

Many a physician throughout the world pretends to be a voice specialist. To all their patients, whatever the affliction involved, they apply the same treatment . . . When the patients feel preoccupied, uneasy, anxious, obsessed, as some singers do, the treatment then is but disguised psycho-therapy, but it is unable to restore the correct coordinations and synergies of the speaker's or singer's voice. Consequently, orators and singers thus treated for months and years just give up because they never recover their vocal possibilities.

"*Antibiotics* are entirely relevant and within the medical jurisdiction for colds or infections that are creating voice disorders. Unfortunately, antibiotics have essentially no basis or relevance for voice disorders that continue following the end of a cold or infection. The postcold or postinfection voice problem occurs in approximately 15 to 20 percent of all voice disorders.

"*Voice rest or voice silence* is another of the leading prescriptive remedies afforded voice patients. Medical personnel as well as lay persons often prescribe voice rest. The presumptive belief for this approach is (1) that the vocal folds tire from natural use rather than from misuse and abuse, and (2) that voice rest will revitalize the tired vocal folds so that a clear and easy voice is produced.

"*Voice rest* is essentially irrelevant to most voice disorders when and if these disorders are caused by voice misuse. Voice rest is misleading to the patient and may become a hindrance because (1) it does not allow the patient to realize he is misusing his voice, since following variable periods of voice rest, the voice usually returns; and (2) following the voice return, the voice is again misused, and further voice rest reveals the extent and severity of progressive voice misuse and/or abuse.

"*Voice rest* is freely prescribed but is seldom observed by those it is intended to assist. Personality effect is sharp and immediate to voice rest, and few patients are able to fulfill the dictum; 'Be silent for a week or two,' or 'Rest your voice for a couple of weeks.' Nearly all patients afforded voice rest have reported that they essentially failed to observe it, except following a surgical procedure and even then voice rest was not complete. Voice rest is usually a mythical panacea.

"*Voice rest* may be relevant following a surgical procedure upon the vocal folds and would then be applicable for a week or two. Longer periods of voice rest following surgery can create voice problems in causing a weakness of unused laryngeal muscles. Some physicians also advise voice rest for a week or so prior to surgery so that the area is not as inflamed and the growth is more clearly defined. Other times when voice rest is appropriate are during severe illnesses or after bouts of yelling, when the vocal folds may be inflamed and possibly thickened."

ADDITIONAL COVER-UP TREATMENTS

Continuing on the subject of palliative treatments, I wrote:

"Other palliative measures, such as gargles, sprays, lozenges, vaporizers, and steam are also essentially irrelevant insofar as voice disorders are concerned. These measures have a slight purpose only in easing laryngeal and pharyngeal pain created by voice misuse and abuse. They soothe the inflamed area for a short period of time. Some symptoms, such as hoarseness, may disappear briefly, but they will usually persist despite palliative treatment. These palliatives merely assuage or mask the pain or irritation in the throat, thereby addicting the patient to repeated doses without eliminating the causative factors and enabling the patient to continue using and misusing the voice. Many a voice patient reports a long history of utilizing these palliative measures, with the essential problem of voice misuse and its attendant laryngeal and pharyngeal discomfort increasing progressively.

"Job change or change of occupation is a prescriptive recommendation afforded the voice patient all too often by unsophisticated medical practitioners and supervisory personnel. For those prescribing such an occupation change the underlying belief is that experiencing voice fatigue is natural to some and indicative of inherent voice weakness either of the larynx or of the physical condition of the patient. Occupations that require little or minimal speaking are recommended for these individuals who experience negative voice symptoms. *What is really needed is a voice change, not a job change.*

"Unfortunately, far too many individuals heed the dictum of job change and become voice hermits. One patient remained at home, seldom answering the telephone, because she was advised that continued voice rest was the only answer to her voice problem. She no longer assisted her husband in the store and the personality effect was severe. Another patient gave up a lecturing career and became a researcher because he was advised to use his voice minimally to avoid voice fatigue.

"*Patients should not be asked to change their personality because of voice misuse.* If a patient is outgoing and dynamic, he should not be told to speak less or to be quiet in order to save his voice. . . . Patients also should not be told simply to speak in a relaxed manner, since what usually happens is that the patient drops the pitch to the basal level, uses little volume, and in the process further misuses the voice.

"*Palliative measures are not curative measures.* They do not eliminate; they merely alleviate. They are misleading to the patient and contributory to the continued voice disorder and personality effect that accrues to a patient with a voice disorder. Palliative measures, nonetheless, continue to be the pervasive measures prescribed by most medical personnel and accepted by most individuals experiencing voice disorders."

THE THYROID GLAND

Case histories of many of my patients include reference to the thyroid gland by their physicians. A surprising number of patients tell me they are taking a form of thyroxin for an under-active thyroid gland.

Another problem involving the thyroid may occur when there is a surgical procedure called a thyroidectomy. A small percentage of patients have voice problems following this operation, due to a lesion of the recurrent laryngeal nerve, which causes vocal cord paralysis. The paralyzed vocal cord may be in one of three positions: median (midline), paramedian (off the midline) , and cadaveric (wide-open). In the first two positions, median and paramedian, I have had outstanding results using Direct Voice Rehabilitation.

PUBLISHED FINDINGS

My findings from a study done at UCLA Medical Center have been published in *California Medicine* and in the *Eye, Ear, Nose, and Throat Monthly.* Of eighteen patients with a paralyzed vocal cord, fourteen were fully recovered, and four were judged to be ninety percent recovered. Time spent in therapy for these eighteen patients was six to eighteen months. Since that time my results with this condition have continued to be good to excellent, and at times, therapy was completed in less than six months.

Some ENT doctors have attempted to perform a surgical procedure by injecting different substances, such as silicone and teflon, in the vocal cord to bring about a closure of the vocal cords. The substances have been changing over the last seventy years because the results are not all that satisfactory. Physicians concerned with a conservative approach have been kind enough to refer patients to me over the years, affording them the option of Direct Voice Rehabilitation alone or in combination with surgery.

In another of my earlier books, *Winning With Your Voice*, I described two patients with vocal cord paralysis. Recovering from surgery to remove a tumor from the thyroid gland, Dr. R., M.D. found his voice was hoarse, lacked carrying power, and faded or failed within a few minutes of conversation. Rather than have a teflon injection into the paralyzed vocal cord, Dr. R. elected to try Direct Voice Rehabilitation. His surgeon, William Longmire, M.D., UCLA Medical Center, referred him to me. I realized, from what Dr. R. told me, he had been having voice trouble before his surgery without knowing it. His voice had been failing and fading, but he assumed this was normal. I concluded it would take a year for him to regain his voice — a better voice than he had ever had. It took him one year, almost to the day. That was twenty years ago. Recently, Dr. R. was on my television show, speaking with the excellent voice he had worked for and obtained many years ago. He said he never gets hoarse or loses his voice anymore. His voice is clear and efficient, yet he still has a paralyzed vocal cord. Not too long ago, I was a guest at his hospital. Some in the medical community found it hard to believe that Dr. R. had ever had a voice problem.

SURGICAL RAMIFICATIONS

Dr. S., Ph.D., in January 1982 experienced a severe

upper back pain and then tingling in his right hand. After some weeks of conservative therapy (placing him in traction), the decision was made that the "slipped disc" in the cervical (neck) area of his spine required surgery to relieve the pressure on the nerves which affected his hand/arm functioning. He awoke from surgery with a paralyzed tongue and vocal cord on the left side.

Dr. S. was immediately referred to an otolaryngologist for what was laryngeal damage during the surgery, he says, and to a neurologist to attempt to discern what nerves were affected and what might be done. An otolaryngologist was ready to do surgery: first a temporary gel-foam injection to give strength to the voice, with discussion about a more experimental nerve transplant operation mostly being done on animals.

During this period, now three months after his operation, Dr. S. had a barely audible voice. Speaking was painful and tiring, with a dryness and raspiness in his voice. Most of his professional activity had to be canceled. He did some teaching, using powerful amplification, but even with microphones, he had to cut back.

After three months, Dr. S. traveled out-of-state for the second time to consult an expert, whose reaction was quite different; he expressed compassion and understanding of what Dr. S. was going through, but he believed that the damage was permanent. Dr. S., he said, would have to face life with a paralyzed vocal cord, although a permanent teflon injection to the paralyzed cord might possibly help to increase the volume in his voice.

As the months wore on, Dr. S. vacillated between depression and coming to accept the possibly permanent condition on the one hand, and on the other hand, a greater desire to exert control over his own health and seek out alternatives, since the medical specialists he had consulted seemed almost unable to help or give any consultative direction other than more surgery.

By now — ten months after his trauma-inducing surgery — Dr. S. was reading everything and anything he could find about voice therapy and voice rehabilitation. At the university where he works, they were using my textbook, *Modern Techniques of Vocal Rehabilitation* (1973). Dr. S. read it and decided to come to Los Angeles and work with me.

Doctor after doctor had told Dr. S. that his condition was hopeless. In one year of voice rehabilitation with his flying in to see me periodically, he recovered his full normal voice. Says Dr. S.:

> Our society has not yet come to realize the pervasiveness of vocal impairment, much less the need to appreciate prevention and rehabilitation and therapy. Helen Keller helped the world understand much about impaired functions and human possibilities. Others have contributed to many advances related to hearing and vision impairment, rehabilitation, and prevention. I do not consider myself an evangelist on this topic. Yet I would be forever grateful if I could contribute minutely to the sensitivity, awareness and training possibilities of persons such as Dr. Morton Cooper. I have witnessed the joy given others as a result of successful vocal work. I know my own

feelings of gratitude to Cooper and to the ability to regain a good voice.

THYROPLASTY

A young lady named Joan suffered a paralyzed vocal cord following a partial thyroidectomy. She was told to see a psychiatrist and accept her severely impaired voice. Declining to do so, she was advised to have a teflon injection. She again declined. She was referred to my office by her ENT doctor for Direct Voice Rehabilitation and has a superb voice today.

Gerald Berke, M.D., Chief of Head and Neck Surgery at UCLA, states: "In the last few years, an outpatient surgical technique has been used that moves the tissues that surround the vocal cords closer together to improve their closure and vibration. For patients in whom one vocal cord becomes paralyzed, surgeons can manipulate the larynx to reenervate the cord." (*Vital Signs*, p. 40)

The Mayo Clinic has taken a similar position: "Today, a new diagnostic technique and a group of surgeries called thyroplasty offer relief to people who previously may have had to adjust to chronic hoarseness due to vocal cord paralysis. The operation tunes your vocal cords by surgically adjusting their tension or position." (*Mayo Clinic Health Letter*, , p. 1)

These surgeries appear to be based on the Isshiki surgical procedure, I believe. However, Dr. Nobuhiko Isshiki who was a colleague of mine at UCLA Medical Center, has written to me to clarify his position: "Surgery is indicated only after voice therapy and when the patient really wants to be operated on."

The so-called hopeless or impossible voice disorders

may not be that at all. The prognosis for having normal and effective voices again can usually be good to excellent, if treated by a competent voice pathologist. Spasmodic dysphonia, paralytic dysphonia, and growths on the vocal cords may be treated by self-help, keeping in mind that these are very serious voice disorders that basically require competent professional direction. A self-help approach may afford you a direction to go in, but essentially professional guidance is necessary for additional assistance.

4

All the Presidents' Voices

We live in a sound society, but few among us have voices that make positive sound impressions. The speaking voice did not become a major means of influence until the advent of mass media: radio, telephone, and later, movies and television. Answering machines have added to the awareness of sound impressions, and the concerns and interest in the speaking voice. Before that, voice impressions were of little interest and consequence. A voice was a voice was a voice.

Have you heard the General Telephone radio commercial with veteran actor George C. Scott? Scott's closing words are: "Put the most powerful business tool on earth to work for you . . . the power of the human voice." It is good. It is strong. But it doesn't tell the whole story. The human voice is simply the most powerful tool on earth.

The speaking voice inherently carries with it many "abilities" — listen-ability, sound-ability, buy-ability, believe-ability, understand-ability, emotional-ability, respect-ability, intellectual-ability, and, above all, Presidential-ability. Indeed, Presidential voices have become important because of the sound impression made upon the public not only by those in office, but also by those running for office.

THE UP-AND-DOWN VOICES OF THE PRESIDENTS

When it comes to troubled voices, how often do we think of the Presidents? Bill Clinton, whose hoarse, raspy voice is frequently heard, may be an exception. But the others? It may surprise you to know that Clinton is not alone. Other of our Presidents did not use their voices to best advantage, and the majority of them suffered for it in one way or another.   Which Presidents had good voices? Which ones did not?

On the following few pages is my analysis of Presidential voices since World War II. The good . . . and the bad.

THE VOICE OF FDR

Of all our Presidents within memory, Franklin Delano Roosevelt had one of the best voices. During the Great Depression and World War II, when America needed strength and hope as never before, Roosevelt gave us just that. He was not physically a strong man, but his voice never betrayed him and it lifted the country to great heights. We became indomitable.

President Roosevelt used the power of his voice through radio and theater newsreels. By far the most effective were his weekly "Fireside Chats." In homes throughout the country, families gathered around their radios to listen and be held spellbound. No pictures, just the sound of FDR's voice coming through the speakers. They were galvanizing moments.

It takes more than words to touch your heart and mind. Franklin D. Roosevelt was a prime example of what a voice can do for a speaker. Although he was an aristocratically reared gentleman, his voice carried a warmth and depth that reached out to the masses, making people at one with him. It is said that FDR's magnetic baritone tenor voice was the golden voice of radio. Indeed, I believe he had the most trusted voice of his time. It was a voice that could be genial and casual, or blistering and energetic, as he wished it to be, depending upon need and circumstance. His voice was essentially laid back, folksy, avuncular. In campaigns he could make his voice as dynamic and driven as any seeking to create emotion and intensity. FDR used his voice as a major instrument of influence, to attract others, to establish himself and his views. Throughout his career in government, as President, his voice was a major means and asset for him to reach out and touch people, influence Congress, and get his views across. FDR knew the value of an attractive, dynamic voice. He was the first of the Presidents to use the speaking voice as a vital source of influence.

FDR made the sound of the voice a key element in persuasion, in conveying information, in carrying his views and programs to the public. Content was essential, but the voice was the ambiance, the honey that allowed the content of that message to be heard.

FDR's voice remained clear and effective throughout his Presidential stay. His was a well-used voice, placed in the mask (the area about the lips and nose), which kept his voice clear, resonant and healthy.

TRUMAN'S "GIVE 'EM HELL" SOUND

Harry S. Truman had a sharp staccato sound, a voice that carried a tone that was in contrast to FDR's, but nonetheless a sound that called attention to the person and got his message through. Truman's voice carried with it intensity when needed, and clarity of tone. Neither FDR nor Truman had trouble being heard or being listened to. Voice was the key in getting them across to the public.

IKE'S LITTLE KNOWN VOICE PROBLEM

Dwight D. Eisenhower presented the public with an avuncular sound. It carried ease and assurance in its tone and presented the listener with a personae not disturbed by national or global events. Eisenhower had a command of voice, though it was not a commanding voice. His voice carried with it the imprint of knowledge and sophistication. It was an open, friendly voice that continued the importance of the speaking voice in the Presidential era of mass media.

I believe Eisenhower was accustomed to giving orders, and aware of the influence of the speaking voice. His experience as a General during World War II allowed him to realize the value of the speaking voice, and its value in carrying a message. However, after suffering a stroke during his Presidency, he presented difficulty with both his voice and his speech.

JFK: A VOICE UNREALIZED

John F. Kennedy gave us a younger, spirited tone, a

voice that reached out to make its points and carried with it the Presidential message. In addressing large crowds, Kennedy attempted to project his voice to the back of the audience by forcing his voice from the lower throat, creating a troubled voice.

Although Kennedy had youth on his side, his public voice was not always used well. He talked better one on one. His conversational voice was more intimate and listenable than was his public speaking voice. FDR, Truman and Eisenhower could talk conversationally if desired in public, particularly at large gatherings, without creating a troubled voice. Kennedy acknowledged his troubled voice by securing a private voice coach to assist him. It is my view that Kennedy did not use his natural effective voice, but relied instead upon the voice he grew up with and became accustomed to, the voice that we knew him to have. He ignored, however, the lower pitches of his voice that had beauty and ease and resonance, elements missing from the voice he presented to the public and to those about him.

In my opinion, Kennedy impressed more with his youth, his energy, his fashion of being, his style, than with his voice. However, his voice was a means of influence, although it was misused in public addresses at times. Both Kennedy and FDR became natural speakers. While Kennedy lacked the experience of Eisenhower, he made up for it with glitz, glamour and his message of hope. If Kennedy had had an FDR voice or a Ronald Reagan voice, how much more effective and influential might he have been?

LBJ'S TROUBLED VOICE

Lyndon Baines Johnson, in contrast to Kennedy, relied upon a deeper, fuller voice as President. In time the focus of his voice, which was in the lower throat, resulted in growths on his vocal cords that were excised by surgery. He was left with a troubled voice which became weaker and less effective after his throat surgery.

Johnson had an accent, as did Kennedy, but Kennedy's accent was considered charming. A Boston accent was Brahmin. Was a Texas accent equal to the Boston accent? That question was not pursued or considered as much as the difference in styles of being and sounding. LBJ didn't use voice as a means and method of influence as did FDR, or later, Ronald Reagan. Voice was not the thing in his time, just as it wasn't the thing with Richard Nixon. Neither Johnson nor Nixon had a trained sound. And neither aspired to make voice talk for them, nor to be an instrument of influence.

NIXON: POTENTIAL GONE AWRY

Nixon's bass-baritone voice was in contrast to the baritone voices of Kennedy, Eisenhower and Truman, and the baritone-tenor of FDR. The fuller voice that is the bass-baritone can carry with it the imprint of authority, experience, awareness and knowledgeability; the bass-baritone voice is a more somber tone, a sound with the authenticity of being. Many seek the bass-baritone voice, but few learn how to use such a voice.

The desire to seek the bass-baritone voice without knowing how to develop it efficiently, if one has such a range, contributes to a great deal of voice misuse and abuse, resulting in troubled, ineffective voices. Richard Nixon did not have the awareness of making the bass-baritone voice work well for him, especially in contrast to the Kennedy baritone as heard in their Presidential debates. The differences in their personalities and in the way they came across in their styles of delivery have been pointed out time and again, but little has been noted about the differences in voice that existed between the two as they campaigned against one another or when both eventually became Presidents of the United States.

Sounding Presidential was well within Richard Nixon's capacity. His bass-baritone, however, in contrast to Kennedy's baritone, carried a sound impression that might not have been particularly favorable, since the bass-baritone carries a sound of misgiving and heaviness, if not used well. It was Nixon's poor voice and his facial mannerisms, probably caused by stage fright, that markedly detracted from his delivery, not his five o'clock shadow.

When President, Nixon became a much better speaker than he was in the debates. His voice was well focused in the mask. Although Nixon brought a fuller, deeper sound to the Presidential office, his voice was never a cornerstone of his presence.

FORD'S "NIGHTMARE"

The Gerald Ford Presidency is a case in point of concern with the speaking voice. Nixon's resignation in the light of the Watergate scandal had Ford filling his term, then running for election himself. As the campaign against Jimmy Carter unfolded, Ford began to pitch his voice lower and lower. It was during the beginning of that campaign, over Labor Day weekend, 1976, that I was quoted in a *Los Angeles Times* interview with Burt Prelutsky as saying, " . . . the politician's nightmare is that he will lose his voice. And it is a legitimate fear because, like actors, they often try for voices far beyond their capabilities. That doesn't seem to be the case with Jimmy Carter. Ford, however, is trying to go lower and adopt an oratorical voice — and, at the very least, he is risking hoarseness and, before the campaign's over, he may blow out all together."

Hearing what Ford was doing with his voice clearly made me aware that Ford wanted a deeper, more manly voice rather than the gentle, friendly baritone he normally used for speaking. He had an even tempered tone, one that did not carry much weight. It was listenable, but not impressive. Increasingly, as his voice began to deepen, I felt he would lose his voice before the end of the campaign.

When I gave my views to Burt Prelutsky, he was concerned and asked if I wanted to allow my prediction to appear in print. I did, and he ran it.

Three days before the end of the campaign, Ford was unable to talk, having gone hoarse. I believe the hoarse voice was caused not by too much talking, but by talking wrong. After this, Burt Prelutsky dropped me a line, saying, "By Jove, you're right!"

Ford didn't have to change his normal speaking voice to a deeper throaty voice in seeking to make his voice manly and fuller. Like so many Americans who want fuller, deeper voices, he dropped the focus of voice, as well as the pitch, and talked from the lower throat — the one spot in the throat nature disallows to be effective and healthy. The lower throat, the deep-throat voice, is the common overall cause of trouble in voices, and the basic overriding cause of hoarseness. Gerald Ford was a leading example.

By giving up the deeper, fuller voice, which he did not use well, and going back to his gentle, lighter voice, Ford regained his normal voice after the election. It wasn't his *real* voice (the lows of his voice were not used). Was voice a factor in Ford's defeat? If he had a Ronald Reagan voice or an FDR voice, could he have carried the day? Perhaps. Granted the backlash at Ford's pardon of Nixon was a key element in contributing to his defeat, would that backlash have happened had Ford sounded differently? I believe Ford's lack of voice lessened his ability to carry off the pardon issue and its consequences, therefore costing him the election. Gerald Ford did not have the voice to pull off controversial or questionable issues of his day. Ronald Reagan did, many times.

CARTER: A VOICE WITH FEW LISTENERS

Jimmy Carter was perhaps the poorer for his voice than any of the recent Presidents. It was thin, nasal, accented with a drawl, leaving him with a voice that lacked influence, believability, sophistication or any of the "abilities" that go with a good voice. Though he took lessons for his voice, it remained post-pubertic and juvenile. His was a voice that left few ears willing to listen to the message. As with Truman, Eisenhower, and Johnson, the voice was not of concern. It was merely a means of presenting the message, the essence of the message being the thing.

REAGAN: THE MOST TRUSTED
VOICE IN AMERICA

In 1980, Ronald Reagan ran for President of the United States. For the first time in several years voice had become a focal point of interest and importance in an election. Hearing Reagan's voice, noting his manner of talking, and then comparing it to Jimmy Carter, I took informal polls of groups I talked with across the United States, as well as on radio and on TV. The overwhelming number of people everywhere told me they were not impressed with Carter's voice and were with Reagan's. Voice had become a key factor in the Presidential race, from what I heard. I predicted early, and stayed with the prediction, that Reagan would win by a voice vote. The economy didn't hurt his candidacy, but I believe his voice was a major influence in the way people perceived him. Reagan's voice was a means of keeping him in the public grace, a key player in his ability to reach out and touch people. He was correctly referred to as "The Great Communicator" for reason; the effective use of his voice was key in his ability to reach out and touch people. The Reagan era was one of voicing it; you can call it the teflon period or anything else. His voice made the negative seem positive. Jimmy Carter's voice did the reverse.

During the 1984 campaign voice again became a meaningful and underlying concern and cause in an election. Aside from the politics involved, people were taken with the voice of Ronald Reagan.

In the first debate with Walter Mondale, Reagan lost on TV. It was said that he appeared distracted while being weighed down with too much factual input. On radio, however, it was a different matter. I noted publicly that radio did not show his fatigue or distraction. Apparently the press agreed with me. An article in the *Los Angeles Times* cited my views and agreed that the radio debate had indeed been won by Reagan.

In the second debate, Reagan was his old, easy, genial self. With his friendly, warm voice and "by golly" demeanor, he won the debate and the election. That debate alone didn't win it all for him, but I believe the cumulative effect of input and stance did. Reagan knew how to talk in public, to talk conversationally without shouting or trying to reach the back of the audience. Mondale lost the sense of intimacy and oneness with the audience. He forgot or ignored the dictum that one-on-one conversational presence is the key to being heard and listened to, if not liked. It is a method and manner Ronald Reagan, the old pro, mastered.

From the feedback and input given me from different parts of the country — I was doing radio and TV shows at the time — I realized that the poor reaction to Mondale's rather high, whiny voice was not local, but national, and that it was a meaningful undercurrent. Months in advance of the election, I predicted on national radio and in newspapers that Reagan would win the election because his voice was a vital influence.

During the final stages of the 1984 campaign, I was contacted by representatives from Mondale's camp requesting material about my expertise on voice. I provided them with my textbook, articles, and my "self-help" book, *Change Your Voice, Change Your Life*. As I was to learn later, Mondale insisted upon remaining authentic to himself. However, he lost in a landslide against the best communicator of our time, a man who could charm by his manner and through his voice. (Mondale's saying he was going to raise taxes in a very definite voice did not help his chances.)

Reagan was made for modern communication and for the American public, which was taken with his voice, his style of delivery, if not his views. Reagan's voice, regardless of his message, had people listening though they may have differed with him.

I believe Reagan replaced Walter Cronkite as the most trusted voice in America. Were Reagan to have had a Truman voice or a Carter voice, would the message have been the same? Would the listenability and believability and reasonability factors have been as convincing and overwhelming and overriding? If Reagan had had Walter Mondale's voice and style, would the masses have tuned in and accepted the message, and the messenger that Reagan became for his views of government?

Ronald Reagan's voice brought to us the friendly, easy tones that allowed us to remain calm and at ease. He had the voice of having been born to the manor. However, earlier in his career as an actor, I heard him talking with a higher, less effective voice. It was not an impressive voice. It did not have the richness, fullness, and warmth that the later years brought to his voice.

BUSH: NO SOUND IMPRESSION

In contrast to Ronald Reagan, George Bush was not one to make a sound impression. The difference in voices was marked, and the contrast sharp. Their messages might well have been similar, but the means of delivering those messages were vastly different. Was it personality? In part, yes. Was it voice? Definitely yes. The voice can make a real difference in the message, and I believe voice made the difference between the full, rich sound of Ronald Reagan in his speeches and the thin, nasal sound of George Bush in his.

George Bush inherited his office, so to speak, from Ronald Reagan. George Bush was not unaware of the sound of his voice during his Presidency. It was characterized as wimpy, nasal, lacking drive, unenergetic. Was that true of George Bush, the person? I doubt it. Bush's voice misrepresented him just as many people are misrepresented by their voices, though they needn't be.

Although George Bush already had years of help with his voice, no change was evident until Roger Ailes put his foot down. Roger Ailes insisted (using the four letter word) that he change by lowering his pitch. I had been on Bush's case, too (though with less colorful words), on national radio, TV, and in print, saying that Bush had a fuller, richer voice, but he didn't use it.

Then, in 1988, during Bush's acceptance speech, a manly, full, rich voice emerged. *That* was the President's natural voice, the voice that George Bush was always capable of using, but never did. Most people, men and women, have that same natural voice — yet never use it.

Thereafter, for some reason, Bush returned to his nasal, thin voice. Only when campaigning against Bill Clinton did the real manly voice of George Bush appear. But it was not consistent. It was now and then, here and there. The nasal, thin tone of the adolescent George Bush returned to prevail, the image of the old voice controlling the impressive tones that might well have gotten him heard, liked and listened to, and even elected, despite the rhetoric and the hoopla.

Nasal resonance is like salt and pepper. Too much and it ruins the meal. George Bush and Jimmy Carter have nasal voices. I believe their messages were diluted in part to the voices.

We basically forgive and ignore a misused voice because our culture accepts the lower reaches of sounds and voices. Gerald Ford was not considered negative when he dropped his pitch and his focus into the lower throat to present a more manly tone. We attributed his loss of voice to voice overuse during his campaign, just as we attributed Bill Clinton's loss of voice to overuse during his campaign. Any misuse is basically overuse. There is really no such thing as overuse if you use your voice correctly and sensibly.

We all experience hoarseness. There were times when even Ronald Reagan became hoarse and talked deep-throat. (I understand he characterized his occasional hoarseness as being due to air-conditioning.) But when he changed his placement of voice to the mask, the hoarseness disappeared. From his years in acting, and his background, Reagan may have discovered that talking in the mask is how he should talk. Or he may have lucked out.

CLINTON'S VOICE: A MEDICAL CONTROVERSY

Bill Clinton's voice is another matter. What he has going for him is likability. He appears to be a genuinely nice and caring man. But his hoarse voice has created more attention, and discussion, than that of any President in modern times.

Clinton's lack of correct voice use has been treated by allergy shots, and though such injections have been provided for some time, the hoarse voice remains. It has been said that his hoarseness will become worse. That view is from allergy specialists, medical people who believe that the allergy-causing factors in Washington, D.C. are worse for the President than those in Little Rock, Arkansas. The medical view of his hoarse voice is that the President is hoarse, will remain hoarse, and possibly get worse because of allergies. Other medical viewpoints have related the President's hoarse voice to diet. He has been advised to give up everything from fries and burgers to chocolate, tea, and coffee. Milk products supposedly create excessive mucus, and since the President clears his throat a lot, medical people are inclined to believe milk products are adverse to Clinton's voice.

It is my view that many of the factors mentioned by the medical advisors are irrelevant to the President's hoarseness. Clinton talks hoarse because he talks wrong — and he will continue to be hoarse until he changes the way he talks, that is, from the lower throat to the mask.

Have you noticed that President Clinton sips water or herbal tea while talking, as though the liquid will relieve his tense vocal cords. It is a known fact that liquid cannot touch the vocal cords because they are protected by three tiers: the epiglottis, the false cords, as well as the true vocal cords close off as soon as we swallow liquid or food. If a substance or liquid should trickle down to the vocal cords, we would not be able to talk. We would choke, badly.

Water or tea — any liquid, for that matter — may help relieve a sore or scratchy throat, but to suggest that liquids help to overcome recurring hoarseness is quaint and fanciful.

Bill Clinton's problem may be reversed simply by

changing the placement of his voice from the lower throat, where he now talks, to the mask, that area around the lips and nose — for starters.

THE PRESENCE OF GREAT SPEAKERS

Great speakers are not born; they are made. Each of the Presidents since World War II has had his moments before a microphone, but only Roosevelt, Kennedy, and Reagan were truly effective speakers. In radio days, Roosevelt influenced by voice alone. In TV days, Kennedy's and Reagan's vocal abilities were embellished by visual properties. Roosevelt, Kennedy, and Reagan knew how to use their voices to scintillate and influence others. They had voices that inspired. Their words and messages were heightened by their sound. Roosevelt was oratorical in public address; Reagan was conversational. Kennedy had a voice presence, and his charisma swayed the populace.

Did you know that most of the very best speakers — *learned* how to use their voices. They, like you, were born with the God-given ability to have good and great voices. But making your true, natural voice speak for you often requires direction. You have to learn whether you should talk higher or lower in pitch, how to focus your voice, and how to breathe correctly for speech. When you have a voice that talks for you, people pay attention. It takes a voice presence to command attention. Anyone who seeks authority, and is moving upward, needs such a voice. That includes executives, politicians, lawyers, teachers, actors, men and women in all occupations. The truth is, *everyone* may have a voice presence at his or her command, but few people know how to use it. Misused, however, that voice can become troubled. If it can happen to our nation's leaders, individuals who have made careers of speaking in public, it can happen to you. Take command of your voice. Be the best you can be.

5

Voice Suicide: Whatever Happened To Voices?

Just as some people dream of Jeanie with the light brown hair (or that certain someone), I dream of voices. These dreams are buzzing with the sounds of Richard Crenna, Richard Basehart and Roosevelt Grier. (Yes, Rosey's talents extend far beyond football fields and knitting needles. He is an outstanding speaker, as well.) On an exceptionally good night I can still hear the voice of Franklin Delano Roosevelt.

Merv Griffin, the popular former band singer turned tycoon, said it best when he had his prime time talk show. Time and again Merv would reminisce about the classic, legendary stars: Gable, Cooper, Stanwyck, Garbo, and so many others. "In those days," Merv would lament, "they had *voices*."

The great stars of the stage and screen did have voices. They had voices that could be easily distinguished, like fingerprints, voices that set them apart, voices with "star quality."

STAR QUALITY VOICES

One word from Bette Davis and you knew immediately that Bette Davis was speaking. From Cary

Grant or Humphrey Bogart or Ingrid Bergman. From Claudette Colbert, James Stewart, George Sanders, Greer Garson, Walter Pidgeon, James Mason or Joseph Cotton. From Orson Welles or Hepburn (Katharine and Audrey). From Brando or Ronald Colman or Don Ameche. They had distinctive, golden voices that worked in perfect harmony with their memorable faces. Just the mention of their names brings to mind the sounds of their wonderfully identifiable voices.

Even supporting players in films had trademark voices. Remember Sydney Greenstreet, Herbert Marshall, Edward Everett Horton, Claude Rains? Remember Thelma Ritter, Peter Lorre, Adolphe Menjou? Each of the studios had its own roster of supporting players with grand and glorious voices. They were stars in their own right, and their voices helped establish the memorable characters they played.

Very few of the current stars have voices that are truly distinctive. They are voices that could belong to almost any of the faces. Hollywood stars were once America's royalty. They had careers that lasted for decades. Now they come and they go, oh, so quickly. And quietly.

THE IMPORTANCE OF VOICE HELP

Whatever happened to voices? Most of the great voices of our time came from the stage, where they were trained to project. When sound came to films, Hollywood called. The names that lit up Broadway soon lit up movie marquees across America. Actors with style and presence. Actors who had magic in their voices.

Hollywood didn't rely entirely on Broadway, of

course. Other performers with special qualities came along from time to time to catch the attention of producers, directors, studio heads and talent scouts. To groom these "finds" for stardom, the studios brought in the finest behind-the-scenes talent available, including voice coaches. Voice was especially important in launching the careers of the newcomers. It was important for the established stars as well if they hoped to make the transition from silents to sound. Those who did not have the "right voices" to fit their styles and images were soon gone. John Gilbert, the great star of silent films, did not last long in talkies.

To help promote the movies, radio played an important part. Many stars appeared on radio as guests on the top comedy, variety, and music shows, as well as in dramatizations of their films. Unlike television, radio brought only voices into America's homes. Easy voice identification was crucial. To be a hit on radio, a person had to have a recognizable speaking voice.

The new breed of Hollywood stars soon had its imitators and impersonators. Suddenly, sound-alikes were everywhere, echoing the trademark voices of Charles Boyer, Humphrey Bogart, Bette Davis, Edward G. Robinson, James Cagney, Katharine Hepburn, Kirk Douglas and so many others. It helped to have a quotable line from one of the star's films. "Come wiz me to zee casbah," said Charles Boyer as Pepe le Moko in *Algiers*. "Come wiz me to zee casbah," said his impersonators in their best Boyer style. It wasn't Charles Boyer, the romantic heartthrob, but it worked. And it helped implant Boyer's mellifluous voice in our minds and hearts forever. (Today, about all we have is Dana Carvey "doing" George Bush, and Phil Hartman as President Clinton, complete with raspy voice.)

Imitation, as the saying goes, is the sincerest form of flattery. But there is a downside to it as well. As I mentioned earlier, it is called "voice suicide."

VOICE SUICIDE

The term sounds ominous, and it is. An individual can inflict severe damage upon his or her own voice — to the point of losing it — simply through long-term voice misuse and/or abuse. The misuse can be deliberate or involuntary. Often a person unconsciously inflicts the damage, but the reverse is also common. The bottom line is, voice suicide is a voice game people play with themselves and others. And it's that voice game that leads to serious voice problems.

Here's how it works. The majority of people do not like the way they sound. They have heard themselves on telephone answering machines, speaker phones, and various recording devices. "That's not *me*," they say, hearing themselves talk. Or: "Do I really sound like *that*?" (Jean Simmons, the star of such classic films as *Spartacus*, *Guys and Dolls* and *Elmer Gantry*, admits that she never watches the rushes of her daily "takes" because they made her feel so uncomfortable. "I don't walk the way I think I walk. I don't look the way I think I look. And I don't talk the way I think I talk.")

HEARING YOURSELF TALK

The voice you hear in your head is not the same voice that others hear. That is because when you speak, the bones in your head literally get in the way, forming a barrier of sorts. Your voice must pass through these obstacles before it reaches your ears. You are too close to your voice to really hear it. Because you are hearing your voice from the *inside,* it is different from your *outer* voice. And it is your outer voice people hear when you speak.

We may not like the way we sound, but we have a definite idea as to how we *should* sound. For various reasons, we become sold on certain voice images, one particular voice or a series of voices. I call them "situation voices." A "put-on" sexy voice, for example, is more attractive than a natural voice to some people. Others want a voice that rings with confidence or authority. For personal or business reasons, or both, they step into a false voice. It is easy to see how attractive it would be for, say a lawyer, to have the deep, confidence-inspiring tones of a Gregory Peck or James Earl Jones type. A salesman would certainly benefit with the melodious voice of a top-flight commercial announcer. Having a voice like Pee Wee Herman or Woody Allen would never do for most of us.

ROLE PLAYING IN VOICE

Many people play out various social roles by voice alteration or voice put-ons. Take the short individual who wears elevator shoes. The extra inch or so may give him more confidence along with a feeling of importance, even though it is more of a psychological lift than a real one. For some reason, many men are convinced that it would be great to be six feet tall, or taller, and have a deep, resonant, commanding voice.

Those attributes are somehow symbolic of manliness and being *macho*.

Little can be done to change a person's measurable height, but within certain limits, the voice can be pitched up or down. Often you may actually develop a voice to fit any voice image you like. Believe it or not, many men and women do have low-pitched voices but do not use them or use them incorrectly.

Men are not alone in playing voice games. Women, too, are guilty. They most commonly try to develop a low-pitched voice because they believe it makes them sound commanding as well as sexy. But forcing the voice down to the lower throat and using a low pitch may, and often does, end in voice damage or even voice suicide.

Voice suicide has never been a recognized problem, despite the introduction of talking pictures in the 1930's. During the so-called Golden Age of movies, and the boom in radios, Americans suddenly had heroes and heroines with glorious voices. The role models for men spoke in deep, rich tones. And the ladies, particularly the sexy ones whom nearly everyone envied, had smoky, velvety voices that seemed to purr. When Mae West lowered her volume and said, "Come up and see me sometime," she sent a message to everyone in the audience. Sex was the message and voice was the medium.

Marlene Dietrich purred her way into our hearts in *The Blue Angel.* Greta Garbo's almost masculine voice simply added to her legendary mystique.

Bette Davis and Tallulah Bankhead weren't particularly sexy, but their throaty voices conveyed enormous strength and determination, rare and envied qualities especially at a time when few women were independent. Lizabeth Scott had been Tallulah

Bankhead's understudy on Broadway prior to her film debut. Scott *was* sexy, and she had Bankhead's husky voice, which made her an instant star. Veronica Lake, fragile and tiny, flirtatiously hid behind her famous peek-a-boo hair and low, whispery voice. June Allyson was like no other girl next door. Her husky and hoarse voice catapulted her to fame.

When Lauren Bacall first started in films, one of her greatest assets was her low, sultry voice. But Bacall didn't come by her voice naturally. Her trademark tones tended to rise when she became nervous or emotional, and cameras put her on edge. Howard Hawks, her director, didn't like what he heard. He insisted that she strain her voice so that it would remain low at all times.

On her own Lauren Bacall drove into the Hollywood hills where she read aloud from a book "in a voice lower and louder than normal." She changed her voice, but I understand she ultimately developed problems with it.

Many of the voices we heard in the movies were contrived by the performers. They had *stage voices*, created for a specific purpose or character, to sell the star or the product. The vocally untrained actors who tried to use those voices at all times were the first victims of voice suicide.

DANGER SIGNALS: THE DIRTY LITTLE SECRETS OF THE SEXUAL SPEAKING VOICE

Little has changed over the years. The times may be different but many of the voices we hear may be self-destructing. Have you heard Suzanne Pleshette lately? Susan Saint James? Brenda Vaccaro? Debra Winger?

Demi Moore? Listen to their voices. Do you hear the hoarse, raspy quality that I hear? Is it the sound of laryngitis I hear — and is it going away? Forcing a low pitch or a put-on voice may be highly destructive, and the trouble usually begins inside the larynx. It is caused by the vibration of the vocal "folds," more commonly known as vocal cords. When someone speaks too deeply in pitch or in focus, the vocal cords may be damaged. Speaking at too low a pitch or using lower deep-throat focus causes tension, then fatigue of the muscles that control the cords. This forces the cords to meet incorrectly as they vibrate, creating functional misphonia (misuse of voice or wrong voice or tired, fatigued voice), the most common type of voice suicide. Continued irritation — or misuse of the vocal cords — may result in benign organic dysphonias, such as nodules, polyps, or contact ulcer granuloma. Voice misuse and/or abuse has even been linked to the onset and development of premalignant growths, including leukoplakia, keratosis, and papillomatosis — big clinical words that spell trouble! Medical studies have even linked voice misuse to vocal cord cancer.

The bottom line, of course, is impairment or loss of voice, because growths on the vocal cords may keep the cords from closing properly during vibration. You should be aware of these symptoms: hoarseness, voice fatigue or tired voice, a voice that breaks when speaking, effortful voice (difficulty in speaking or in being heard), and a repetitive, on-going need to clear the throat.

Much of what I have been discussing has concerned what I call "the dirty little secrets of the sexual speaking voice." (Madonna is a good example. Wrote columnist Liz Smith of "The Material Girl" and the character she played in her 1992 film, *Body of Evidence:* "Madonna pitches her high, much-criticized voice down to low, femme-fatale cadences.") In a broad sense, it all relates to voice put-ons and the games we play with our voices.

THE "CONFIDENTIAL" VOICE

I am reminded of a teacher who came to me needing help with her voice. In the classroom she liked to speak in "a confidential voice," which she said appealed to her students. But the voice she chose to use did not have carrying power, so she pushed it down into her lower throat. Her voice tired easily.

The confidential voice can be most effective in some situations. It sounds intimate and gets attention. But in a classroom full of students, it is necessary to slightly increase volume. To do that you must have firm control of midsection breathing. You also need to raise your pitch somewhat, because the higher pitch carries better with less effort. This lessens the confidential effect somewhat, but can be successful nevertheless.

When I met Don, an actor, back in the 1980's, he talked as if he were under water. His voice was gargley and garbled. He had nodules on his vocal cords, which he called "kissing nodules," because every time he tried to speak the nodules vibrated and "kissed."

Hoping to cure his problem, Don saw a speech clinician, who practiced indirect therapy. (Indirect therapy advises the patient to use relaxation, to stretch the neck muscles, to use the "h" sound before each word, to drink lots of water, etc.) When that therapy failed to help him he turned to his doctor.

Dr. Ed Kantor told Don that he had nodules. Don insisted they be removed. "I've got to get rid of them so

I can work," he said. "I need my voice."

"That's drastic," Dr. Kantor told him, "and the last thing we do here." Instead, he advised a non-invasive direct approach and referred Don to me.

"I love Dr. Kantor," Don admitted to me. "The man is a surgeon who doesn't believe in surgery. He felt I could be cured by direct therapy, and he was right." Within a month Don was once more going out on auditions. He had gotten his voice back, and he kept it — for a number of years. His new problem began when he started talking in a deep voice from his lower throat, admittedly trying to impress with "deep, dulcet tones."

Says Don, "The only time I talked properly was on stage, when I breathed from my diaphragm and projected my voice. On film I didn't. I found I could whisper so I used low tones. It was devastating. I really wrecked my voice."

By the time Don visited me again he had developed spasmodic dysphonia. "I sounded like I was being strangled," Don remembers, "like somebody had their hands around my throat."

Like Don, the majority of patients with spasmodic dysphonia have had longtime misuse of their voices, which resulted in tired voices. The condition definitely is not an overnight sensation. And like Don, others had had nodules, polyps, or contact ulcers early on, which were eliminated by Direct Voice Rehabilitation. Years later, after reverting back to their old, bad voice habits, they developed SD. (Some patients have had nodules or contact ulcers along with the SD.) True, there are exceptions to long-term voice misuse, such as Gayle. Because Gayle had a cold, her condition came on just like that!

Don now says he doesn't think about his voice

anymore. He's cured of spasmodic dysphonia. "I just talk. And it all came through therapy and practice, practice, practice — like a musical instrument, which the voice is." Don emphasizes that his voice is richer and more resonant. And he has full control over it.

Because Don was playing games with his voice, he developed SD. He had an voice image of himself, and that image projected a low pitched voice from the lower throat. Voice game playing is hardly unique. We all do it. I was guilty myself at one time.

A PERSONAL EXPERIENCE

It wasn't until I went to college that I discovered I sounded like Bugs Bunny. When I said "hello," people said "goodbye." That was painful in itself, but the deepest hurt was yet to come. Two well-meaning speech coaches offered help by telling me that they could remove the "tinny" sound from my voice. All I had to do was speak lower, from deep in my throat, and it would disappear. That "sound" advice came after I landed the part of a 53-year-old man in the college production of a play called *Both Your Houses*. Because of the character I was playing, I was constantly being reminded to speak in deeper tones, using the lower part of my throat.

As the rehearsals continued I began losing my voice, and since I was also in the university chorus (singing bass), I noticed that my singing voice was deteriorating at the same rate as my speaking voice. It got to the point where I couldn't even talk in regular conversation. The eventual result was chronic laryngitis. I was losing my voice and I didn't know it.

After graduating from college, I volunteered for the

Army, feeling that I owed my country two years of service, having been given a scholarship to college. In the Army I served in the American Forces Network as an announcer. My voice was continuing to present problems throughout this time; talking was becoming more and more of an effort. I tried to find help for my voice, but no one seemed aware of why my bass-baritone voice was troubling me. It sounded fine to others, but my throat hurt when I talked.

After I had been discharged from the Army, my failing voice was closely scrutinized by a dozen specialists, but none of them could help me. In the process, I was given drugs and told that my problem was from sources unknown to them. I was also told that what I had was genetic. One doctor suggested the possibility of cancer. I refused to accept the medical diagnosis for my hoarse, troubled voice and was sent to a psychiatrist.

As I sat in a darkened office, the psychiatrist repeated words that I had heard before. My problem, he said in his troubled voice, might be genetic. To make matters worse, he insisted that additionally the problem was in my head.

By chance, I received help in overcoming my troubled voice. Friedrich Brodnitz, M.D., helped me to realize I was talking wrong. But it was two broadcasters, Stan Burns and Paul Sherman, of WINS in New York City, who were instrumental in giving me the practical direction of focusing my voice with midsection breath support. But none of them talked about the new voice image vs. the old voice image.

The traumatic experience led to my choosing a career in voice and speech pathology. It wasn't until then that I began to realize that the field of voice was as lacking in answers as the doctors had been. Even so,

I wasn't discouraged.

My goals in life had changed. It became my greatest hope to rescue others from the uncertainty of the long, long ordeal I had gone through.

At Indiana University, at Stanford University, and at UCLA, I continued to teach myself how to use my voice correctly. Taking voice science, physiology of the larynx, and an extensive number of voice courses did not change my voice, although I had insight into the mechanism of voice. That came when I discovered through practicing with my own voice how simple the use of the efficient and right voice is, with the focus around the lips and nose (the mask), and midsection breath support, together with a new voice image. After about ten years of working on my voice, I had developed a rich, full voice that would not hurt nor tire no matter how long or under what circumstances I spoke. I had found the secret to the speaking voice. Now people assume I was born with my present voice.

HOW VOICES DEVELOP

We are not born with good or great voices. Voices are like bodies. The potential is there, but they must be developed. Just as you weren't born with a good or great voice, neither were you born with a poor or troubled voice. That, too, is developed, yet without your knowing it.

Between the ages of twelve and fifteen, our voices change from a boy's voice to a man's voice, or from a girl's voice to a woman's voice — a kid's voice to an adult's voice. In my opinion, fifty percent of us retain a kid's voice as we mature and, therefore, talk in a wrong voice as adults. It happened to me, and it happens to many others.

Michael Jackson has a kid's voice. So do Mike Tyson, Tom Selleck, Fred (Mister) Rogers, and former President Jimmy Carter. As I hear it, they have voices that have not grown with them — voices that are too high, too thin, too light, or too nasal.

"Talk like a man." We've all heard those words, if not said directly to us then to someone else. *Talk like a man!* Many men don't. They sound like kids.

What about the ladies, grown up women who sound like little girls? Melanie Griffith comes immediately to mind, as did Jackie Onassis. They have kids' voices that give them a sound of helplessness, vulnerability, and innocence.

Some women's voices have a "baby doll" sound, the stereotype voice of the "dumb blonde," the bimbo. Jayne Mansfield had it. So did Marilyn Monroe.

Kids' voices are what I also call "in person" voices. These voices so completely misrepresent the individuals that unless you talk to them face-to-face you would never guess they were speaking. Or take them seriously.

The kid's voice in adults is one end of the voice scale. The real danger zone — deep-throat-- is the other, because it affects approximately twenty-five percent of us. Deep-throat is the rough, gravelly sound of Henry Kissinger, Lloyd Bentsen and, yes, President Clinton. The President may have made being hoarse fashionable, as Barbra Streisand quipped not long ago, but being hoarse is one fashion that will be extremely short-lived. Losing your voice, and being unable to speak, is not fun — nor good for your health.

Keep in mind: when you speak incorrectly, either too high or too low in pitch, with improper tone focus and/or inefficient breath support, you put too much pressure on your voice mechanism. This creates a lopsided balance of muscles that can end in growths on the vocal cords, even premalignancies or spasmodic dysphonia.

We are all creatures of habit. This is easily demonstrated by our normal daily life from the time we awake to bedtime. It would be inefficient to have to think about each activity and behavior, so we develop habit patterns and do a substantial amount of our living unconsciously by habit. We get into a voice pattern and stay with it, believing that is our only option. It is not. No one can put a voice in you, but you may be shown how to bring out your God-given *natural* voice, a voice that has power, appeal and star quality.

SEEKING COMPETENT VOICE HELP

Voice misuse and/or abuse should be avoided. This applies to everyone. If you recognize the symptoms of voice suicide, first consult a knowledgeable throat specialist interested in the speaking voice. Then you can try my self-help voice program for a brief period to see if the symptoms abate. If not, seek competent, professional training from a qualified voice clinician or a speech pathologist who is trained in voice.

As discussed in my textbook, *Modern Techniques of Vocal Rehabilitation,* all clinicians are not alike in training or orientation. In 1982, Charles W. Vaughan, M.D. stated: "Effective voice therapists are rare. . . . Some speech therapists, teachers of singing, and voice scientists are skilled in voice therapy; many are not. The physician must recommend a specific therapist who is known to be knowledgeable and effective."

Again, I repeat, seek professional help for voice disorders, but seek out a knowledgeable voice clinician or voice pathologist. The advantages far outweigh the costs, especially when you realize that a properly trained voice never really tires or lets you down.

6

Speaking of Kids

Young people are not immune to voice problems or disorders. Like adults, they can misuse and abuse their voices too, and frequently do.

Several years ago, following a guest appearance on a local radio talk show, I met with a group of young students. The youngsters were taking what was called a radio class. After being introduced to the class, which was made up of a broad ethnic mix of whites, blacks, Asians, and Mexican-Americans, I was shown the textbook they were using. From that, I was told, the students were learning how to use their voices. It was then they began to ask questions. When I heard them speak, I thought, "Heaven help them." All had poor voices, except for a few. These young males tried to act so macho in front of their classmates, yet sounded so juvenile with their high-pitched, nasal voices.

What are the symptoms of a young voice going wrong, and how can you spot them?

There are actually three ways to tell. Perhaps the most obvious is by listening to the child. Auditory symptoms include hoarseness, breathiness, a voice that skips or breaks, loss of voice, reduced vocal range, and inability to be heard, among others.

Sensory symptoms experienced by the youngster include a sore throat, a scratchy throat, a "lump" in the throat, coughing, throat clearing, and cording (lower throat muscles tense and knot).

Visual symptoms, as seen by a laryngologist during laryngoscopy, are most often the last to be detected. These symptoms may be inflammation or edema of the vocal cords or organic lesions on the vocal cords, such as a nodule, a polyp, a papilloma, or a contact ulcer.

CAUSES OF VOICE PROBLEMS IN THE YOUNG

What brings on voice problems at such a young age? The cause is basically the same for a child as an adult: voice misuse and/or abuse. Any number of factors may be responsible, such as lack of voice knowledge, imitation of inadequate or unsuitable voice models (inappropriate voice image), poor voice hygiene, singing in groups, and/or change of voice at puberty (males especially).

Contributory causes may include: (1) emotional problems; (2) medical factors, such as allergy, postnasal drip, hay fever, infected tonsils, and sinusitis; (3) a hearing problem; and (4) a cold or upper respiratory infection.

The lack of voice knowledge, imitation of inadequate or unsuitable voice models (does your child try to imitate his or her favorite rock singers?) and singing in groups may create voice misuse. That is because the child is using the wrong pitch level with an improper tone focus in combination with too much volume.

Most children, I find, have a voice image, which is the positive and negative feelings and reactions toward a given voice. The voice image determines what kind of voice a child likes and uses or dislikes and does not use.

Another major influence on youngsters, in addition to rock stars, are athletes. Yet sports stars are notorious for misusing their voices. They may look big and brawny, brimming with physical strength, but many of them sound weak and wimpy. They have trained their bodies, but not their voices.

Youngsters may imitate cartoon characters, whose voices do not fit them, and they may also imitate crazy sound effects. An interesting side note is that a number of voice-over actors abuse their own voices.

Poor voice hygiene is one of the most common causes of voice abuse. Just as an adult will shout at ball games, letting runaway emotions erupt through his or her voice, so will a child. But youngsters have more outlets for yelling, screaming, and shouting. They also shout on school playgrounds, on the street, in backyards, even at home, whenever and wherever the urge hits them. They talk with too much volume in cars and buses, and compete with noise, such as TV, stereos, and traffic sounds. The subsequent voice the child uses may be strained because of an edema or inflammation of the vocal cords.

ADDITIONAL CAUSES

Voice problems may begin at puberty because the boy does not know what pitch to use when the larynx increases in size. He may drop too low in pitch; he may attempt to retain his former high pitch (falsetto voice); or he may drop the pitch slightly, but not far enough.

Falsetto voice, also known as juvenile voice, occurs when the pitch of the boy's voice does not drop sufficiently and remains at a high pitch level. Thus, the habitual pitch (pitch used) is above the optimal pitch (natural pitch).

There are two viewpoints regarding the use of the falsetto voice as Alan Satou, M.D. and I discussed in "Psychiatric Observation of Falsetto Voice" (*The Voice*, Feb. 1968). One view is that the voice is used unintentionally and that the individual must be shown the correct pitch level through voice rehabilitation. The other view is that the young man is intentionally continuing to use the falsetto voice because of psychological factors.

Part of voice rehabilitation is brief voice psychotherapy, that is, discussion of what the voice image is and why the individual may be using a voice that is inappropriate.

If the falsetto voice is used after voice rehabilitation, that is, after the voice clinician finds the correct voice and affords therapy to the patient for a reasonable period of time (one to six months), the problem may be considered to be psychological in nature. In this case, psychotherapy or psychological counseling must be afforded the patient after, or concomitant with, voice rehabilitation.

Emotional problems may contribute to a voice disorder if the emotional difficulties cause the child to yell frequently or to be depressed, often resulting in a forced voice.

Medical factors (allergy, postnasal drip, etc.) may be contributory to the onset, if not the continuation, of a voice disorder only in some cases. Usually, if the child can be taught to use the voice correctly, he/she is influenced minimally by these medical factors. A hearing problem is a factor only if the child has a bilateral severe hearing loss.

The common cold or upper respiratory condition

contributes to the voice disorder in that it may cause the child to begin using a lower throat voice or a deeper pitch due to the inflated vocal cords. Voice misuse can begin if the wrong voice is continued following the cold.

HELP FOR YOUNG VOICES

It is important to know that help for voice disorders in children is available, and the prognosis for recovery is good with the help of a qualified clinician. The parents' role in the recovery process is important as well, since "relationship therapy" may be used with most youngsters.

Relationship therapy is when the parent, or parents, serve as a clinician at home between therapy sessions. However, teenagers may not respond to relationship therapy as successfully — or at all — and may work only with the clinician.

Because voice disorders and voice abuse are becoming increasingly prevalent among young people, it is vital for parents to be on the alert for the warning signals or symptoms.

7

Hope for Hopeless Voices

Dana Carvey and I have something in common. During an appearance on *The Tonight Show* he told host Jay Leno that he listens to voices. I listen to voices too, but not for the same reason. While Carvey, a brilliant comedian and impressionist (his George Bush and Ross Perot are right on the money), listens to pick up tonal qualities and nuances in order to impersonate famous personalities, I listen for poor and troubled sounds. And the sounds are everywhere.

Many doctors have a *medical* orientation. I suggest they should stop only looking and start *listening,* also. Too often a doctor will look down your throat and take tests, but he may not be listening to your voice. So you go on talking as you do, complaining as you should, and getting worse.

People often ask me how I know a healthy voice from a problem voice. I tell them I can hear it. You may learn to feel and hear it, too.

With a healthy voice, an individual's vocal cords are clear. The properly used voice remains strong and efficient, as the day goes on.

The problem voice can be shrill, nasal, thin, guttural, too high-pitched or too low-pitched. It can also be harsh and irritating, difficult to listen to, and unappreciated.

SIGNALS OF ON-GOING VOICE PROBLEMS

Actually, the majority of people who misuse their voices are totally unaware that they have a voice problem. All too frequently, these people clear their throats when talking. They have trouble being heard, and their voices fade or fail. They constantly are asked to repeat themselves. And they experience neck aches and pains. These symptoms are signals of trouble ahead.

The voice often is one of the most abused and misused modalities of the human body. Countless numbers of Americans suffer from laryngitis, hoarseness, throat clearing and coughing, as well as tired, failing, and troubled voices. They don't realize that these symptoms may be caused by using the wrong voice.

Nature has ways of telling you something is wrong with your voice. Throat clearing is the most common symptom of voice misuse. Hoarseness is another. Your doctor may prescribe drugs to ease these symptoms, but are they listening to your voice? This question might be asked of most physicians who treat patients with symptoms of voice problems.

Hoarseness and laryngitis (inflammation of the larynx) have many different causes, including smoking, the common cold, and various medical problems. However, the most common factors that create and prolong everyday hoarseness and laryngitis I see, are voice misuse and abuse. If you use the voice effectively, you should be able to talk as much as you want, under normal circumstances. I do not agree with Lawrence Altman or Gerald Berke, M.D. Lawrence Altman, in *The New York Times* (April 14, 1992), wrote in a column titled, "Laryngitis Like Clinton's Is Common Among Politicians," that the main cause of laryngitis is overuse of the voice. He also stated that: "The standard treatment for chronic laryngitis is resting the voice, drinking lots of fluid and using humidifiers." According to Gerald Berke, M.D.: "Smoking, voice overuse or indigestion [often this means acid reflux] are common causes of laryngitis, a condition that can usually be treated effectively by stopping smoking, resting your voice, watching your diet, or taking a short course of medications." (*Vital Signs*, p. 4)

Hoarse voice is often nature's way of telling you to change the way you talk; it is a message that has not been taken in by many doctors. They believe the hoarse voice is essentially due to diet, reflux, allergy, postnasal drip, sinusitis, or overuse of voice, but not basically to misuse of the voice. Many doctors do not understand how misuse of the voice occurs, and they don't listen to voices, per se, to understand that wrong use of the voice comes from the lower throat, or deep-throat. Medical treatment suggests, more often than not, voice rest, medications, change of diet, allergy shots, Zantac or Prilosec for reflux, change of job or personality, or just live with it. Among the fashionable treatments is drinking lots of water as reported by Jane Brody in *The New York Times* (May 25, 1989) and as recommended in written instructions to voice patients by UCLA Medical Center Speech Pathology Department and by Kaiser-Permanente Medical Center Speech Pathology Department. All of these treatments ignore the basic over-riding cause of hoarseness — the wrong use of the speaking voice. (Unfortunately, I find *The New York Times* is inclined to report the medical view as though it is the only view.)

I do not ask hoarse patients to rest the voice. I help them change the voice from hoarse to clear by a change in pitch and a change of tone focus from the lower throat to the mask. In case after case I see, I do not find the medications, voice rest, or diet change helping the voice until the voice has been changed by Direct Voice Rehabilitation. Although it would be better if the patient does not smoke for his own general health and the health of his voice, I insist on "no smoking" only in very select cases.

HELP FOR HOARSE VOICES

If you suffer from hoarseness or laryngitis without medical cause, on a regular or continuing basis, you know that it does not go away easily. You have tried rest, pills, steam, gargles, shots, even voice rest, and still it persists. Can anything be done? Yes, indeed.

You must learn to focus your voice with normal volume. Do not try to compete with noise. Most Americans, men and women alike, do not use what is natural to them. Instead, they seek the lows of their voices or talk too high pitched, essentially in both cases talking in the lower throat. They lack the right direction, the right focus in the mask, and succumb to hoarseness and laryngitis. Laryngitis is irritation of the vocal cords. Hoarseness essentially comes from talking wrong. Throat clearing is often an accompanying symptom.

In an article titled, "Is your voice hoarse? It could be just talk" in *USA Today*, I pointed out that hoarse voices respond to direct voice help (a change in focus, pitch, and breathing) and allow the voice to showcase the speaker. Such a voice also allows the speaker to talk as much as he/she desires under normal use (not competing with noise). Those who wish to talk in competition with noise are shown how to do it, as with coaches. Jim Harrick, the UCLA basketball coach, is an excellent example. I helped him to find his voice, and I showed him how to effectively use his voice in conversation and in noisy situations. Years back, I helped Bill Sharman, when he was coach of the Lakers, regain his voice which he had lost by shouting.

THE STRESS FACTOR

Adrenaline is our body's natural stimulant. It helps to push us in our drive to succeed and gives us a competitive rush. But there is a downside to all that energy, especially in professional life. It used to be called "nerves." Today, it is *stress.*

Tension and stress can do more than create or contribute to a voice problem. If not controlled, the problem can steadily worsen, particularly if other factors such as smoking, drinking and illness are involved. The good news is that you need not have a stress-related voice problem. You may rescue your voice even if you are in a stressful situation.

Stress can make your body tense, and put you on edge. Your voice may respond by going too high or too low in pitch, often hugging the sensitive lower throat. It becomes rough and gravelly. Words crack in mid-sentence. Clearing your throat doesn't help. You sound awkward and tentative. Your voice is not one of confidence.

The key is to learn how to control your natural voice. Some people do it instinctively. Others must learn.

Most people let stress go to their lower throats, and it may show in their voices through a squeezed, tired, troubled sound. A stressed voice may strain careers and personal relationships. Physically, it may damage your throat and result in nodes, polyps, contact ulcers, and worse. It may also lead to a strangled voice — one that sounds like someone is choking you as you talk. President Clinton's voice, more often than not, has the sound of stress as he talks.

Speaking in a relaxed way isn't easy when you really are not relaxed. The secret is to be aware of your focus, and your breathing. Let the sound produced from the vocal cords reach out and touch your lips and nose, and resonate there. A properly used voice should relax you, knowing that you sound strong, dynamic, confident. You don't have to relax the entire body to sound good, but knowing that you sound good should help you relax.

A daily physical workout, I find, helps me face the day relaxed in body and voice. I recommend it for patients who need to relax and reduce stress.

TALKING THROUGH TENSION

You may relax your voice by humming. Sir Victor Negus, a noted ear-nose-throat doctor, used the humming technique to help his voice patients. Margaret Greene, a well known British speech pathologist, helped her voice patients, also, by humming exercises. Constantin Stanislavski, the legendary acting coach, discussed how humming could produce the feel for the right voice. Frank Sinatra is said to hum to warm up his voice. Humming is just as easy to do when you are among people as it is to do when you are alone. When other people are around, a near-silent hum or a hummed response ("um-hmmm") should help you place your voice correctly. With practice, you should soon have the feel of it.

People in stressful situations tend to hold their breath. It can happen at any time, no matter where you are. Under stress your body stiffens and breathing becomes irregular; you may even hold your breath periodically.

When Warren visited my office, he commented that speaking on the phone makes him tense. Unfortunately, he is on the phone a lot at work, and his voice gives out. I asked him to count from one to ten. When he did he held his breath.

"Why did you do that?" I asked.

"I don't know," he responded.

"Is that how you talk on the phone at work?"

"I guess so," he replied. "I hadn't thought about it."

I told Warren to have his secretary take messages and hold the calls until later in the day when he felt he could concentrate on his voice. He looked at me as if I were joking. When he discovered I wasn't, he tried my suggestion. It worked. In fact, it worked so well that he is now able to talk through his tension.

It may work for you too. But not everyone has a secretary to run interference, or the luxury of being able to hold calls until another time. The important point, however, is to remember to use your natural voice. To do that, you must breathe regularly and from the midsection.

When you breathe, the shoulders should not move up and down, and the upper chest should remain still.

Movement should essentially come from the waist area or midsection. Your stomach should move out when you breathe in, and as you talk, it should move in smoothly and gradually. Breathing from the midsection allows the body to relax and eliminates tension from the throat.

To see if you are breathing correctly, lie on the floor on your back. Place one hand on your chest and the other on your stomach. Imagine you are going to sleep. Breathe gently and easily with your mouth slightly open. Your stomach should move; your chest should show little or no movement.

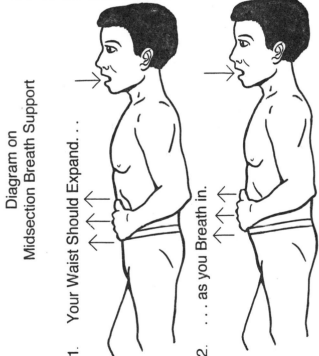

Diagram on
Midsection Breath Support

1. Your Waist Should Expand. . .

2. . . . as you Breath in.

Once you have the feel of this correct type of midsection breathing, practice it in a standing position and finally in a sitting position. The next step is to talk using midsection breath support. Practice breathing in and talking on the out-going air for a few minutes each hour throughout the day until it becomes natural and routine. When you are trying to get midsection breath support, you may find that your rate of speech slows down. This is only temporary. Once you achieve control of your breath for speech, your normal rate will return.

MAKING STRESS WORK FOR YOU

When you learn to use your voice correctly, stress may actually work *for* you, instead of against you, no matter who you are or what you do. That extra throb generated by nerves may turn a so-so voice into a captivator, making it even easier to listen to — and persuasive.

The lesson, then, is: Do not try to hide your nerves. Use them. Let your voice speak out, not down. Speak up, but approximately two to three notes from the bottom of your range if you are guttural. Use the "um-hum" technique. Modulate your voice. And breathe evenly from your midsection.

As I mentioned earlier, the common cold can also lead to voice problems by lowering the pitch and bringing the focus down to the lower throat. The tendency for an individual with a cold is to protect the voice by keeping the pitch and focus down. Unfortunately, since that voice really isn't the natural or normal voice, it grows tired and hoarse, or it fails, creating laryngitis.

When a cold strikes, try to keep your "normal, before-the-cold" voice going. If the pitch drops, bring it back up to your right pitch level and mask focus. The question is, how do you remember what your pitch level was before the cold started?

The exercises in Chapter 2 will help you relocate your correct pitch and tone focus. If you have any doubts use the Cooper Instant Voice Press with the "hmmm-hmmm-hmmm" and the "ah-ah-ah." Next time you have a cold, test your voice and your voice agility in this simple way. It may keep you talking, feeling better, and doing better.

Our voices have a way of telling us when they are going wrong. Listen to the warning signals: the coughing, throat clearing, voice fatigue, raspiness, and so on. If your voice feels bad, it probably *is* bad and will not become better until you learn to talk correctly.

A QUICK VOICE HELP REVIEW

To review for you: To work properly the voice has to be used in focus — like a camera. When the voice is out of focus, its energy level is sharply curtailed, so you have to push more to talk. That makes talking tiresome for you and puts a strain on your listeners. Talking should be effortless.

To find your natural sound, the voice must be focused in the mask and not in the vocal cords, which produce a thin sound. People who squeeze their voices from the lower throat wind up with troubled voices, and possibly more serious problems. When you talk with nasality these problems do not occur. You simply create "ear pollution" as well as "sound pollution."

It is so easy to focus your voice in the mask area by practicing the simple humming exercises, along with the Cooper Instant Voice Press. Focusing your voice may take only seconds, but learning to use your voice correctly in conversation takes time and practice. The effort will be worth it. Most can *hear* the difference between the old habitual voice and new natural voice as well as *feel* it.

Does your voice need to be refocused? Does your pitch need to be changed? Does your breathing need to be improved? Most voices do need these changes. Voice misuse can result in negative auditory and sensory symptoms.

During my long career as a voice and speech pathologist, I have found that certain symptoms are related to the misuse and abuse of the speaking voice. At the start of therapy, I ask all my patients to fill out a Voice Evaluation Chart, which pinpoints negative sensory and auditory symptoms indicating a wrong voice. They are asked to fill out the form again at the end of therapy. This, along with visits to a laryngologist for an examination at the beginning and end of therapy, and as needed during the therapy process, allows me to follow their progress. Playbacks of the patient's new voice are equally valuable.

Here is a chance for you to evaluate your own voice. Take a few seconds to check the sample Voice Evaluation Chart below. You may be surprised by the number of symptoms that apply to you.

VOICE EVALUATION CHART

NAME _____ DATE _____

SENSORY SYMPTOMS   ELIMINATED
__ 1. Non-productive (without relief),
        repetitive throat clearing   __
__ 2. Coughing   __
__ 3. Progressive voice fatigue following
        brief or extended voice usage   __

___ 4. Acute or chronic irritation or pain in or about the larynx or pharynx ___
___ 5. Sternum pressure and/or pain ___
___ 6. Neck muscle cording ___
___ 7. Swelling of veins and/or arteries in the neck ___
___ 8. Throat stiffness ___
___ 9. Rapid voice fatigue ___
___ 10. A feeling of a foreign substance or a "lump" in throat ___
___ 11. Ear irritation, tickling or earache ___
___ 12. Repeated sore throats ___
___ 13. A tickling, tearing, soreness or burning sensation in the throat ___
___ 14. Scratchy or dry throat ___
___ 15. Tenderness of anterior and/or posterior strap muscles ___
___ 16. Rumble in chest ___
___ 17. Stinging sensation in soft palate ___
___ 18. A feeling that talking is an effort ___
___ 19. A choking feeling ___
___ 20. Tension and/or tightness in the throat ___
___ 21. Chronic toothache without apparent cause ___
___ 22. Back and neck tension ___
___ 23. Headache ___
___ 24. Mucus formation ___
___ 25. Arytenoid tenderness ___
___ 26. Trachael pressure ___
___ 28. Pain at base of tongue ___

AUDITORY SYMPTOMS
___ 1. Acute or chronic hoarseness ___
___ 2. Reduced voice range ___

  __ 3. Inability to talk at will and at length
         in variable situations   __

  __ 4. Tone change from a clear voice to a
         breathy, raspy, squeaky, foggy, or rough
         voice   __

  __ 5. Repeated loss of voice   __

  __ 6. Laryngitis   __

  __ 7. Pitch too high; pitch too low   __

  __ 8. Voice too nasal; voice too throaty   __

  __ 9. Voice comes and goes during the
         day or over a period of month   __

  __ 10. Clear voice in morning, tired/foggy
         voice later in day   __

  __ 11. Missed speech sounds   __

It would be interesting to see President Clinton's chart. How do you think it would compare to yours? While the fate of over 250 million people may not hinge on your decisions, and you may not be quite as visible, you do share at least one thing in common with the President: the need to communicate — in a voice that is healthy, strong, durable, and listenable.

Betty had such a need. Betty is a Los Angeles attorney. Here is her story, in her own words.

"My problem started as a cold and a sore throat in February of 1990. I wanted to use some of my sick time to take a few days off, but my supervisor wouldn't let me. So I kept working, forcing my voice. When I went to court I could barely whisper. I had to hold up signs.

"I didn't see a doctor right away. My voice would come back, I felt. The same thing had happened to me briefly years earlier when I was a law student. I had lost my voice then, and it did come back.

"It wasn't until one of the judges, whom I met in the coffee shop of the building where we worked, told me I should see a doctor, that I did. At St. John's Hospital in Santa Monica I was put on disability and referred to a doctor. My husband had to make all the arrangements since it was impossible for me to be heard or understood.

"The doctor, an ENT, at first seemed to be good. He gave me antibiotics but no extensive tests. He thought my condition would go away if I kept my mouth closed for a week. I did, and it didn't. My doctor then advised me to see a speech pathologist as well. He sent me to one, whom I visited once a week. She told me no talking without taking a drink of water after every few words. I also learned that I was sitting wrong and talking too fast. 'You have to pay attention to these things,' she said. When I questioned her therapy, she added, 'We (speech pathologists) all do the same thing. It works.'

"While all this was going on, my performance review came up at work. Taking so much time off had been bad enough. Now I received a bad review for being unable to talk. Because of that I tried going back to work on a modified schedule. I shouldn't have done that. The added tension brought on the worst stress headaches. On top of that my throat ached. The pain was incredible. If I came to work with only the slimmest portion of a voice, it was soon collapsing.

"Through all of this, I was still seeing my ENT. During one visit he said, 'I think you should see a psychiatrist. There may be something in your past, dark secrets.' I couldn't believe he would say such a thing. My head throbbed, my throat ached — and he wanted to send me to a psychiatrist?

"I don't know where I heard Dr. Cooper's name first,

but it kept coming up at various times and places. I was told that Dr. Cooper handled all the cases that were considered incurable and hopeless. 'That's me,' I told myself. 'Dr. Cooper's the man for me.'

"I called Dr. Cooper and he agreed to see me. I'll never forget my first visit to his office. He listened to my pathetic attempts at talking and said, 'We'll get your voice back.' Then he sent me to another ENT, Dr. Harvey Paley. I thought, 'Here we go again,' but I was wrong. Dr. Cooper simply wanted a medical opinion as to what was wrong with me.

"It turned out that I had bowed vocal cords. I had so totally destroyed my voice that I had pushed the cords apart. Blown them out!

"I worked with Dr. Cooper six days a week for the next four months. It wasn't easy because we had to undo all the wrong I had done in misusing my voice. And I won't say there wasn't any pain in trying to get the uncurved muscles of my vocal cords back into proper shape. But the rehabilitation exercises worked, and they were not invasive and had no side effects.

"Now I have my voice back. It is strong and healthy, and I have no pain. No sore throat muscles. I wouldn't be speaking again if it weren't for Dr. Cooper and Dr. Paley. I can only say, if you have a voice problem, get the *correct treatment* early on. Don't wait. Don't let it progress as I did."

DIRECTION, PATIENCE AND WORK

Betty was a conscientious patient who stayed with her exercises day after day, so she felt positive things happen. A percentage of patients don't want to do something for themselves. They want the easy way, the quick fix, as I mentioned earlier. To change a long-term misused voice requires direction, practice and work to change what is wrong to what is right.

I liken it to a diet. If people, who are overweight and go on a crash diet, don't want to change their eating habits, they revert back. My patients who fail are essentially unable or not willing to put out the effort to make the change and use the right, efficient voice.

Failure to recover is cultural in part — an unwillingness by patients to change or alter their voice image. They don't know that they control this condition and they can't conceive that they are misusing their voices.

"How long will it take to improve my voice?" That is one of the first questions I hear. My response is usually in the form of a question: "If you are turning the key in your lock to the left, and I tell you it must be turned to the right to open the lock, how long will it take you to change the way you turn the key?"

The answer should be obvious. I can tell you *how* to do it, but it is up to *you* to *make* it *work.* As the saying goes, it all depends on you.

Some patients are dedicated and quick to learn. Others are unwilling to practice and cooperate. Their attitude is that the therapy must be done for them, not by them. Still others believe that by attending the therapy sessions the voice problem will be resolved with token effort. Token effort usually results in minimal improvement and, more often than not, failure.

Generally speaking, however, it takes only *seconds* basically to find your true, natural voice but then, many *minutes* of practice each day to maintain it. To make it habitual — that is, to speak naturally and spontaneously in your new voice — will take some work and time. It is impossible to put all patients into one category and demand they recover quickly or at a specified pace. It has to be at their own pace. Overcoming a voice habit pattern of any type may be difficult. As Mark Twain wrote in *Pudd'nhead Wilson. Pudd'nhead Wilson's Calendar:* "Habit is habit, and not to be flung out of the window by any man, but coaxed down-stairs a step at a time."

I believe that the prognosis is excellent for most voice disorders, but the patients have to cooperate. Some patients are so resistant to change that they will never recover. Most are willing to change.

Contrary to prevailing opinion, hopeless voices are not basically hopeless. It is no secret that I differ with my colleagues and medical associates in treating misused and abused voices, including tired, fatigued, weak voice, nodules, polyps, contact ulcer, spasmodic dysphonia, bowed vocal cords, and paralytic dysphonia, as well as other voice problems. With Direct Voice Rehabilitation in my office, the prognosis is excellent in most cases, but there are no guarantees. The successful results with thousands of recovered patients speak for themselves.

8

Change Your Voice,
Save Your Life

We all make excuses in life, even when it comes to our voices. The majority of people honestly believe there is nothing that can be done to make their voices sound better. One of the most common excuses I hear is, "But I've talked like this all my life."

People who misuse their voices are almost always unaware that they have a voice problem. It isn't until something goes wrong, and they start losing their voices, that they seek help. And while it is almost never too late to receive help, the longer you wait . . . well, you know the rest.

Lucille Ball needed help with her voice. (Remember how rough and scratchy she sounded for a time?) So did TV and radio personality Shadoe Stevens, talk show host Joan Rivers, and author Harold Robbins.

My program of Direct Voice Rehabilitation is essentially similar, but with appropriate modifications, for all types of organic, neurological, and functional disorders. Organic voice disorders include nodules, polyps, and contact ulcers, which are benign lesions. Neurological voice disorders include Parkinson's Disease and cerebral palsy. Functional voice disorders, which I find are related to voice misuse and abuse, include tired voice, spasmodic and spastic dysphonia, and bowed vocal cords; these conditions, if untreated, could well be a prelude to organic voice disorders. In functional voice disorders, the voice shows wear and tear, and is inefficient without organic or neurological factors being present, indicating that voice misuse or abuse basically is occurring within the normal laryngeal structure. The greatest number of cases in this category normally result from the simple fact that the patient is talking incorrectly. In other words, the patient is doing it to himself or herself.

MIND-BODY TECHNIQUES

In Direct Voice Rehabilitation, the first step is locating and identifying the optimal or natural pitch level and range as well as the correct, balanced tone focus. A simple method, which I use, is my "um-hum" technique. With this exercise, the patient is told to simply say "um-hum" spontaneously and sincerely as if agreeing with someone in conversation. If the "um-hum" is produced with the proper pitch and tone focus, the patient should feel a slight buzz or tingle in the mask area around the lips and nose, as in humming "Happy Birthday."

Another simple, total mind-body technique that may allow for immediate correct and natural pitch and tone focus is this: The patient bends over from the waist, keeping the legs straight, letting the arms fall forward toward the floor with the head hanging downward in a relaxed position with the chin on the chest. As the patient is in this position, a hum ("um-hum") or "oh" is sustained. This position often breaks the body tension and the body armor--which is the habitual, but not natural, use of the voice--allowing the real voice to come forth.

Still another approach is to have the patient hum (staying in the bent chin-on-chest position) while the patient or clinician gently jiggles with the fingers in a staccato fashion on the patient's midsection or higher (at about the level of the solar plexus). Or in another exercise, the clinician may also gently jiggle with the hands on both sides of the patient's midsection (at about the bottom of the rib cage) in the staccato fashion while the patient is humming and is in either an upright or bent-over position. "Jiggling" with the fingers or hands may be likened to jogging in place in aerobics. (These are variations of the Cooper Instant Voice Press, which was described earlier. As mentioned earlier, do not try these exercises if you are pregnant or have medical problems involving the stomach or area of the solar plexus.)

ON HEARING YOUR NATURAL VOICE

All of these approaches may allow the real or natural voice to be heard. It must be emphasized that almost all patients initially react negatively to the new voice by saying that it is too loud or that they are shouting. Reassurance that the new voice — or the natural voice — is normal in volume must be made by the clinician, by other patients, and by others outside of therapy.

To review, if the patient does not have midsection or central breath support, the correct breath control should be developed. The patient is instructed to lie on his or her back, with one hand on the chest and the other hand on the midsection (waist). He or she is told to breathe easily through the nostrils as though resting or going to sleep. The patient must experience the midsection moving gently out as the chest remains stationary. The exercise is then repeated while breathing through the mouth while in the same supine position.

The next step is to practice this exercise while standing, breathing first through the nostrils and then through the mouth. The last step is to practice in a sitting position, again breathing first through the nose and then the mouth. Keep in mind, we basically breathe through our mouth when talking.

Following the identification and establishment of the new pitch, tone focus and breath support, the patient must become accustomed to the sound and feel of the new voice. He or she also must then learn to use the new breathing technique together with the new voice in a controlled therapy environment, which will be carried over to outside situations.

As I mentioned earlier, the length of time required for voice rehabilitation depends on such variables as the ear of the clinician, the "feel" of the voice in the mask and the ear of the patient, and the cooperation of the patient. A survey of patients seen over a thirty-year period indicates good to excellent results with those who completed the voice rehabilitation process.

VOICES THAT SING

Over the years, I have worked with some internationally famous singers from the various stages of musical entertainment, including Stevie Nicks (lead singer for the rock group Fleetwood Mac), Diahann Carroll (multi-faceted singing star of Broadway, motion pictures, nightclubs and television), and Jerome Hines (famed star of the Metropolitan Opera). Mr. Hines, in fact, insisted on mentioning his one-time voice problem in his book *Great Singers on Great Singing* (Doubleday, 1982) and inviting me to contribute a chapter in this book.

He wrote, in part:

"In the mid-1960s, when I was suffering from a severe vocal problem, I consulted Dr. Morton Cooper, a most successful speech therapist in Westwood (Los Angeles), California. The short time I spent with him provided insights that were very important to my vocal recovery. . . . (It was) Dr. Cooper who pointed out that much of my trouble had its roots in incorrect speaking habits. Giving heed to this has also been most valuable."

The singing and speaking voices should have basically the same pitch level, range and tone focus. A marked difference between the singing and speaking voices should tell you that one of the two voices is not being used properly.

Amateur singers frequently do not sing in the proper range, either because they are unaware of their optimal pitch range or because they are assigned incorrect pitch ranges to use in group singing. The untrained singer also uses too much forced volume and usually lacks good midsection breathing for tone support. This weakening of the singing voice often results in hoarseness, laryngitis, poor range control, voice breaks, and volume problems.

A LECTURER'S TROUBLED VOICE

Let me tell you about some patients who are not singers. Dr. F. began to lose his voice in early 1973 while he was lecturing at a university in Iran. At first he felt a strange sensation in his vocal cords, but they gradually weakened until he was barely able to speak. An ENT doctor in Tehran prescribed antibiotics, which failed to help. That summer he traveled to England to see a voice specialist. "That trip was of no use," says Dr. F., "and my problem became worse."

He struggled with his voice until the following summer when he flew to the United States to consult with his cousin, a medical pathologist who was then doing research at a prominent medical school. His cousin recommended Dr. W., then added, "If that doesn't work out, see Dr. Hans von Leden in Los Angeles." Dr. W. did not work out. According to Dr. F., "His prescription for me was odd. He had me chew a golf ball and, for that, one of my teeth broke apart."

In September 1974, Dr. F. flew to Los Angeles. It was in Dr. von Leden's office that "my problem was first diagnosed as spastic dysphonia. After extensive examination he referred me to Dr. Morton Cooper."

On September 12, 1974, Dr. F. came to my office. Although he had been told about his condition and its severity, I emphasized to him that it was not that unique, nor hopeless, as many people are led to believe. By using my Direct Voice Rehabilitation exercises, he could indeed regain his speaking voice in time. How long that would take was impossible for me to project. I knew nothing about his dedication and willingness to practice.

Dr. F. remained in Los Angeles from September 1974 to July 1975. During this period I saw him twice a week. Dr. F. admits: "In the beginning I was pessimistic toward the outlook of the treatment, but after a few months I found that my voice was going to its natural level without slipping back too low. Dr. Cooper's treatment was so effective that after eleven months I was back to my real voice. And it has remained strong, not losing ends of words or sentences.

"Dr. Cooper's treatment was a new experience in my life as I regained my natural voice and also my career. Personally, I owe my voice to Dr. Cooper. Of course, I worked very hard during the period of rehabilitation, exercising his methods of first humming words and, later, sentences, and breathing correctly.

"Finally, I have been able to teach regularly every semester since September 1975, carrying a full load of 15 hours per week on the average. I am forever grateful to Dr. Cooper and his rehabilitation program for making it all possible."

Dr. F.'s voice remains excellent twenty years after DVR.

THE ADVERTISING EXECUTIVE

Rachel is an advertising executive. She had been having problems with her voice and throat for approximately eight years when she came to see me. She had been to four different doctors — ENT specialists — who told her she had a variety of problems ranging from a vivid imagination to allergies, sinusitis, and postnasal drip. One doctor recommended that she read psychology books on self-esteem. She was also told that she had "globus hystericus," a term defined by the medical dictionary a "a lump in the throat in hysteria and other neuroses." This essentially means the problem is said to be in the mind, not in the throat. I have seen this term numerous times in medical reports ascribing the lump in the throat or feeling of a foreign substance in the throat to hysteria, when in actuality the patient may feel the lump and may experience the foreign substance feeling because they are squeezing the voice from the lower throat. A throat examination does not reveal a lump or a foreign substance, but tension produced by wrong placement of voice creates the sensation of a lump. After completing voice rehabilitation patients have reported to me time and time again that the "lump" is gone. (See symptom chart.)

Another physician informed Rachel that she had swollen nasal membranes. It was the mucus draining from these membranes, he said, that gave her the sensation of having a lump in her throat. She received a shot of cortisone in her nose to "combat the inflammation." For the next two years she returned regularly to the doctor for cortisone injections in her nose. Says Rachel, "It got to the point where I'd wake up every morning *believing* I had a lump in my throat."

Why the doctor continued to give Rachel shots over an extended period when they weren't helping her, I don't know. Then, again, why would he have told her she had swollen nasal membranes? The only answer is that the doctor wasn't listening to Rachel. He was only looking for something to treat. If he had known about symptoms of voice problems he would have known that many people who are misusing their voices have the feeling of a foreign substance, such as a lump, in their throats.

The treatment for Rachel's non-existent lump continued for nearly three years. At one point a scope was inserted down into her throat. On the doctor's recommendation a piece of tissue at the back of her tongue was removed because it appeared to be enlarged. Rachel says she had some relief for about a month before the pain returned.

Because Rachel's voice condition seemed to come and go with the seasons, then worsen for long periods, it was believed she had an allergy. She was given a variety of medications, plus an inhaler spray. She was on drugs for about a year. Says Rachel, "The pain didn't worsen. In fact, I started feeling better so I stopped taking the medication. Then, gradually, everything came back. This time I thought, 'Oh, well, I really do have allergies' and started in again with the drugs. But they didn't work like they did before."

RACHEL'S "TIRED VOICE"

Rachel was back where she started. Her throat ached as if a foreign body were lodged in it, and her voice was rough and breaking. Rachel's case is typical and symptomatic of a condition called myasthenia laryngis, a big term for "tired voice." If not corrected, tired voice can lead to voice suicide. Rachel was on her way.

You've heard people after a long, hard day or an extended period of talking. Their voices sound like sandpaper. They not only look tired, they sound tired. Tired voice comes from talking down in the lower throat. Instead of talking into the mask — around the lips and nose — they let their voices drop into the danger zone. They do it because they want authority, status, position. Or they don't know any better and just let their voices sink. As their bodies tire, so do their voices.

"I let my voice drop because I wanted a strong voice," admits Rachel. "I thought it made me sound older, more powerful. I didn't realize I was doing it, or how I got my voice down there, but I liked what I heard."

By the time Rachel came to my office she had been from doctor to doctor, enduring throat pain, along with difficulty in speaking, for eight years. "After one day with Dr. Cooper," she says, "I could feel the pain lessening. He started me with humming exercises, then 'um-hmm' and counting with 'um-hmm.' He worked on my breathing, on raising my voice and on getting it focused correctly. I could actually feel what was happening in the mask, where it belonged. And I didn't feel any pressure in my throat as the air passed through. I was forming words, making sounds, without putting a lot of effort into it."

Rachel didn't particularly like her new voice when she heard it played back to her. She thought it sounded strange, more like a little girl than the image she had created for herself. She also had a confession of sorts. She liked to sing. When she started singing lessons her teacher told her to sing in the mask. Singing gave her relief, she said. Every time she ended a lesson her voice was higher than when she began. That higher, natural, feel-better voice stayed with her about an hour on lesson days. Then she'd revert back to her troubled voice without realizing why or how. "Singing and talking were two entirely different things to me," she said. "I never connected the two. Now it makes sense . . . focusing in the mask *and* breathing properly. When I sang, my stomach went in. When I spoke, it went out. I was doing all the wrong things before, speaking in the lower throat and reversing my breathing, things I didn't do when I sang."

While Rachel is thrilled to have a strong, healthy voice again, and to be living without pain, she cannot help but remember the wasted years she spent trying to find help, and the thought makes her angry. "The doctors are all too ready with their needles and knives and drugs. I saw four of them and not one knew what was wrong with me."

MISDIAGNOSIS: IS IT A VOICE PROBLEM?

Rachel is not an isolated case. The condition that sent her to a series of doctors is all too common today; millions of patients across America may be misdiagnosed or undiagnosed. These patients may be given checkups to see if anything is medically wrong, but they usually receive a clean bill of health. That doesn't mean there isn't anything wrong. All too often there is a voice problem. The patient is talking in the wrong direction, from the wrong area — the danger zone — so the cause goes untreated and the patient continues to suffer, physically and mentally.

I have said it before, but it bears repeating: many doctors do not hear the problem because they are not trained to listen. I am not knocking the doctors. It isn't their fault. The medical profession is to blame for ignoring voice by not making it part of required training.

JOE'S "SEXY VOICE"

Joe had a serious voice problem, which he lived with for forty years. During most of that time he thought he was "talking sexy." It wasn't until he realized his voice was killing him that he sought help. As Joe explains, "I used to have a very deep, raspy voice. People used to say, 'That's a sexy, deep voice, Joe.'

I thought that was great, so I went along with it, never knowing it was doing me harm, causing problems."

For Joe, speaking deep-throat seemed natural. He had been talking that way for so long he didn't know there was any other way. He even admits that if anyone had criticized his low, authoritative voice when he was younger, he probably would have ignored the criticism. But warning signals were ahead. "I'd get tired talking," he says. "If I had a conversation that lasted for ten or fifteen minutes, I felt like I'd run around the track. Now I wish I'd had voice training with a good speech therapist when I was a kid."

When his doctor advised surgery for polyps on Joe's vocal cords, he took his doctor's advice and went ahead with the surgery. His voice not only didn't improve, it became worse, very hoarse. This time Joe's doctor told him to seek out a voice clinician. "I went every week," says Joe, "but I was never taught the proper mechanics of speaking. Instead, he concentrated on my breathing, and that was about it."

Two months before Joe came to my office he had a second surgery for polyps on his vocal cords. Following that operation his doctor said to him, "You don't want to keep having surgery because that could result in more problems, very serious problems, such as premalignancies and cancer."

At sixty-five years of age, Joe began Direct Voice Rehabilitation. He was talking from his lower throat when I first saw him. His voice was down. It grated when he spoke, much like a highly advanced geriatric voice — only worse. I told Joe he was wearing his voice in the wrong place. "If you don't wear your glasses in the right place, you can't see," I said. "It's the same way with your voice."

It took one session for Joe to find his right voice. He

then followed with exercises every day, concentrating on the correct placement of his voice so that it would become natural for him to speak correctly without thinking about it. Now Joe says, "I've had people call me on the phone and hang up when I answer. They can't believe it's me. Even my doctor can't get over it. He says I'm like another person!" Joe simply needed to get his voice focused and to learn diaphragmatic breathing.

SUCCESSFUL RECOVERIES FROM
ALL WALKS OF LIFE

There are so many success stories like Joe, Betty, and Rachel, all documented. Zelda, a teacher, was diagnosed by Robert Feder, M.D., a well-known laryngologist in Beverly Hills, as having spastic dysphonia. After undergoing an intensive six-month program of Direct Voice Rehabilitation, she recovered her speaking voice. Zelda had had polyps on her vocal cords fifteen years prior to the onset of spastic dysphonia; the polyps were eliminated in three months by Direct Voice Rehabilitation. She attributes the onset of the spastic dysphonia to stress and a desire for a lower pitched voice. Although she still has stress she now knows how to handle her voice.

Rabbi Alan was diagnosed at the UCLA Medical Center with spasmodic dysphonia in early 1989. Following a program of Direct Voice Rehabilitation, he was referred back to UCLA for a phonatory analysis and was found to be speaking normally. At that time, he says he was told he could not have had spasmodic dysphonia because there is no recovery from it. He was told that the original diagnosis must have been wrong.

In 1996, three years after completing DVR, Rabbi
Alan speaks with a normal voice 99% of the time. In a
recent letter I received from him he says that the final
1% of SD continues to diminish. In his description of
his voice problem, he writes that "self-expression
manifests through the vocal mechanism. If the vocal
mechanism is blocked, the self is stifled. And if the self
is stifled, the vocal mechanism is blocked! And so one
spirals down into SD."

He continues to explain, "You have discovered how
to reverse the spiral, from a descending to an
ascending one. First you unblock the vocal
mechanism, and the self begins to become more free.
The increasing freedom of the self further unblocks
the vocal mechanism! And so on. Reflecting back on
the process of my own healing, that's how it seemed to
progress for me."

Marjorie was diagnosed at the UCLA Medical Center
as having severe spastic dysphonia eight years ago. She
was unable to produce a single word. She declined
surgery. Through a program of Direct Voice
Rehabilitation over a period of years, she recovered
her normal voice. She is now able to talk under the
conditions and in situations she once avoided.

Lisa was diagnosed as having spasmodic dysphonia
by a well-known laryngologist in Los Angeles. She was
treated by antibiotics but did not improve. A six-month
program of Direct Voice Rehabilitation helped her to
recover a normal voice. Five years later she appeared
on a TV program with me, reaffirming that her voice
remains excellent.

I could go on and on introducing you to patients
who have recovered from the most severe voice
problems with Direct Voice Rehabilitation. These are
people from all walks of life and spanning a wide

range of ages, whose voices simply gave out on them. They were losing their voices, but they went on for years without knowing it.

Have you listened to your voice lately? Do you like what you hear? If your tape recorder isn't broken, your voice is. Actually, when you come right down to it, your recorder — or your answering machine — may be your best friend. Where else can you find out that your voice isn't working right for you? Your friends won't tell you.

Listen to the warning signals. Do you clear your throat a lot when you talk? Does your throat ache? Does talking tire you? Is it difficult or effortful for you to speak? Does your voice get weak or fade in and out? Does your voice get all used up during the day? Is it clear, or gravelly? Do you become hoarse after talking for a while or by the end of the day? Do you have an irritation around your throat, as if you have a foreign substance or a lump in there? Do you have a feeling of tightness or tension in your throat? The well-used voice should not have these negative voice symptoms.

There is a widespread mistreatment of our voices. The cover of this book lists some of the common symptoms of voice misuse and/or voice abuse, including sore throats, throat clearing, weak voice, poor projection, pain when talking, strangled voice, voice strain, hoarse voice, lump in throat, tired voice, deep-throat voice, hurts to talk, throat tension, and nasality. (Voice Evaluation Charts are in Chapter 7.) You may have additional problems or define your symptoms in different terms. If you will, add to these lists by writing down your symptoms and sending the list to me. Your voice can be symptom free.

Talking should be as easy as 1, 2, 3. It should come naturally. It should give you confidence and make you feel secure. Your voice should never hold you back. It should — and can — help make you a better person, in every way. Your voice can be your fortune. We live in a sound society.

If you want a healthy, more effective speaking voice, isn't it time you did something about it?

9

The Madness of Medicine

Remember *Network*, the 1976 movie that satirized the world of television? One of the great moments from the film had Peter Finch, playing anchor-man Howard Beale, the "mad prophet of the airways," shouting the now-famous line: "I'm mad as hell, and I'm not going to take this anymore!"

Sometimes I feel like Howard Beale. Sometimes I feel like going to the window, opening it wide, sticking out my head, and yelling, "I'm hungry as hell, and I'm not going to listen anymore to the doctors. I want a Big Mac, and fries, and chocolate. I want tea and coffee, and all the good things in life. I am tired of being fed myths!"

Food is not really the enemy. Some foods consumed at some time or another may affect the voice, such as an allergic reaction to shrimp, spicy foods, etc. Food does not cause most people to become hoarse on a continuing basis, but the wrong way of talking *does*. You, the person, are doing your voice in. In my many years of practice, I have been told by patients that they are allergic to coffee, milk, caffeine, chocolate, and dairy products, yet when I show patients how to use their voices properly, food may no longer be a basic issue. Just be a friend to, and with, your voice. The point is, when you talk right, in most cases you may talk as much as you want — without any advice from well-meaning but misguided doctors.

CONFLICTING BELIEFS

My being at odds with the doctors is not a sudden happening. Over the years, by accident not intent, I have managed to offend very powerful people in the fields of speech pathology and medicine. Early in my career when I was on the staff at UCLA Medical Center, I was privileged to work with Dr. Joel Pressman, Chairman of the Head and Neck Division, and with other knowledgeable faculty members including Dr. Hans von Leden, Dr. Alan Nahum, and Dr. Sam Pearlman. While I did therapy with patients, my ear told me the overwhelming majority of voice problems were caused by too low a pitch and forced lower throat resonance, not by too high a pitch, which was believed at that time. After producing excellent results for three years with my approach to voice, Dr. Pressman called me into his office to tell me I was doing everything ass-backward, but nonetheless, my results were excellent. Three years after this incident, Dr. Pressman again spoke to me, assuring me at this time that since my results continued to be excellent, that the field I was in was ass-backward, and that I should tell the field what was going on. Dr. Pressman wrote of my services that I was the best speech pathologist he knew.

When I received my Ph.D. from UCLA, I was invited to join the faculty as an assistant clinical professor in the Head and Neck Division. My dissertation had involved a clinical program of voice rehabilitation, over a period of three months, for eight patients with biopsied papillomata (premalignant lesions) of the vocal cords. Although a review of the literature indicated that vocal abuse and irritation were possible etiological factors, as were virus infection and hormonal imbalance, the main methods of treatment were medical, immunological, and surgical. The lesions were reduced or eliminated by Direct Voice Rehabilitation in four of the eight patients, thus indicating a link between voice misuse and abuse and papillomatosis. The study was supervised by the medical faculty and the results were affirmed by the faculty, who did before-and-after laryngeal examinations. Dr. Pressman was astounded at the results. This study was published in the *Journal of Speech and Hearing Disorders* in 1971.

EARLY SUCCESSES

My dissertation was originally prompted by a case I had seen at the Marion Davies Children's Center at the UCLA Medical Center. It was there I worked with a twelve-year-old boy whose medical chart stated he had papillomatosis of the vocal cords. His voice was produced from the lower throat; the quality of voice being severely hoarse. He was also a yeller. His growths disappeared after about one year of Direct Voice Rehabilitation.

Two biopsied cases of papillomatosis were also seen by me. The first involved a general manager of a large pharmaceutical company who came to me after surgery because of his hoarse voice. He realized he had been talking in an intimate, confidential voice for years as part of his job. After a period of many months, his voice was produced in the mask and not in the lower throat. Approximately five years after the completion of therapy, he appeared on public television, describing and demonstrating his excellent voice. The other case involved a physician who had had three surgical procedures to remove the growths. He reported that he used his voice as a weapon, forcing his voice from the lower throat. He was seen twenty years following the completion of therapy, reporting that he had never had a recurrence of the problem. Margaret C. L. Greene, one of the foremost speech pathologists, has written in her textbook, *The Voice and Its Disorders*, 5th edition, that: "A case confirming Cooper's view that speech therapy can reduce or even eliminate papillomata in children was encountered by Greene in Auckland." (p. 246) She describes the case of a nine-year-old boy whose papillomata were reduced in number and in size following voice therapy.

My findings regarding papillomatosis conflicted with the beliefs of a local surgeon who had insisted that surgery was the only answer and who had performed almost 200 (two hundred) surgeries on one patient for this problem. With a program of Direct Voice Rehabilitation, the patient improved. Physicians apparently still do not see the relationship between voice misuse and abuse and papillomatosis from my experience.

After Dr. Pressman's untimely death, the new chairman of the Head and Neck Division at UCLA had an orientation to voice problems that was not the same as mine. It was time for me to leave.

MEDICAL PROOF

Sometime later I testified in a court case involving a patient who had gone from a benign lesion to a malignancy, requiring a laryngectomy. The patient was seeking Workers' Compensation since he had lost his voice as a result of having to yell on his job. The expert ENT physician testifying for Workers' Compensation said there was no proof that a relationship between voice misuse/abuse and malignancy of the vocal cords exists. I presented medical studies indicating that voice misuse and abuse can lead not only to benign lesions but also to malignancies. After I presented the evidence, the physician recanted his testimony. At a subsequent meeting of the Otolaryngological Society, I ran into this well-known doctor who was highly critical of my testimony against his orientation.

In 1977 at the Houston Medical Center, I was part of a national program that included two colleagues. In introducing me to the group, one of the individuals called me "the fastest gun in the West." I took that as a compliment at first. Then he went on to describe his colleague's patient who suffered from a hoarse voice and had not improved during nine months of therapy. In a challenge, of sorts, he appeared to me to doubt my ability to help the patient locate his natural voice in seconds, which I find is often possible.

The patient, a minister, was brought to the podium where he offered a few words in his hoarse, troubled voice. Contrary to what was expected of me, I found the minister's natural pitch and correct tone focus in only seconds. It was then that a person in the audience spoke up. What I did, he said, was a fluke. My answer to that individual, and to the audience, was: "On a slow day it takes but ten seconds." My remark apparently didn't set well with this member of the audience, who turned out to be Wilbur Gould, M.D., the founder of The Voice Foundation, which publishes *The Journal of Voice*, directed to otolaryngologists, speech-language pathologists, singing coaches and voice scientists.

CLOSED EARS — AND MINDS

At the same meeting, one of the ENT doctors heatedly questioned the validity of the papillomatosis study. These experiences, I believe, have demonstrated a difference in orientation toward the treatment of voice disorders. "The powers that be" do not care to consider my approach to voice, and have closed their ears to what I have had to say for the benefit of their patients and themselves.

Over the years, trying to lead the fields of medicine and speech pathology out of the Dark Ages in regard to voice rehabilitation or voice improvement has been an on-going battle. It is inconceivable to believe that in these times a medical doctor will advise a patient to use his tongue, instead of a brush, to clean his teeth as a possible cure for a troubled or abused voice, or write a prescription directing a patient to chew on a golf ball to improve his strangled voice. Another patient was advised to change his liquor from scotch to bourbon, and when that didn't help, to have surgery. Still another was instructed to stop eating peaches. All too often, the simple, corrective techniques are overlooked in favor of more complicated, outdated and bizarre methods that are irrelevant to the problem itself.

It is almost as if these professions do not want to advance or help the patient. When years of successful rehabilitations have proven that it basically takes only seconds to determine someone's real voice, why are others in my field so taken aback by the simplicity of my approach?

Criticism from some colleagues is not new and comes as no surprise to me. In 1980 the prestigious *Wall Street Journal* ran a lengthy, front-page article chronicling the success of my voice techniques, under the headline, "How Norton Simon, With Help, Finally Found Voice He Had Lost." While the article was ninety-five percent positive, including Mr. Simon's comment, "it's really miraculous," it did note, by an unnamed source:

Mr. Cooper's methods are somewhat suspect among his fellow speech pathologists. Most of them maintain it takes months to analyze the causes of the speech difficulty before treatment can begin. Mr. Cooper says that by first finding the natural voice,he can often solve the whole problem.

To repeat again, *finding* the natural voice is not difficult nor time consuming. *Learning to use and maintain* the natural voice requires time and cooperation.

THE POLITICS OF VOICE

The field of voice rehabilitation, I find, is rife with politics. In 1984, I was interviewed by *Los Angeles Times* reporter Beverly Beyette for a story about the successful recovery of my patients through the use of Direct Voice Rehabilitation.

One afternoon, shortly after the interview, Ms. Beyette called to tell me that the story had been pulled. It seems that during the course of Beverly Beyette's research, she was told by four different sources in the field that I had never been published in medical or scientific journals, nor had I ever had peer review of my findings.

My list of published credits, books and other writings, fills two-plus printed pages and I immediately forwarded this information to Ms. Beyette. Shortly thereafter a comprehensive and complimentary article appeared in the *Los Angeles Times*, discussing my philosophy, my techniques, and my positive results with patients with several types of voice disorders as well as with spasmodic dysphonia. Beverly Beyette had done her homework. Unknown to me, she had interviewed former patients who were willing to go on record telling their stories of voice recovery. Although the article included several negative comments by one source, who remained anonymous, Ms. Beyette did acknowledge my credits and peer review at such highly acclaimed hospitals as Walter Reed and Cedars-Sinai, and before audiences of peers at the American Speech-Language-Hearing Association (ASHA) and the California Speech-Language-Hearing Association meetings. "At Odds with Establishment" was the headline above the story. A more appropriate title might have been "Establishment at Odds with Reality."

It appears to me that ASHA was also downplaying the success of Direct Voice Rehabilitation for severe spasmodic dysphonia even as early as 1980, as indicated in the *Wall Street Journal* article:

He (Dr. Cooper) even claims to cure Spastic Dysphonia, a serious organic vocal condition in which the patient can barely gasp a few words at a time. Most therapists say the condition requires medical treatment rather than speech instruction alone. An official of the American Speech-Language-Hearing Association says, "Many pathologists who listen to Cooper's 'before' tapes think his patients have a less severe malady."

Not so. The spasmodic dysphonic cases I have worked with were extremely severe. Lately patients have come with medical diagnoses from the leading medical centers throughout the United States, including UCLA Medical Center, the Mayo Clinic, and Stanford University. For example, in the previously mentioned Beyette article, she reported:

Dr. D. started having voice problems 10 years ago and was diagnosed at Stanford University as having Spastic Dysphonia, probably incurable. "I was finally discharged after being told they'd done everything they could," he said.

Dr. D., who is assistant vice president, academic affairs, University of _____, remembered reading a Morton Cooper book and sought him out. "It took me a year of working with him to really catch on to the techniques," Dr. D. said, "and another two years to work them into everyday speech." Today, he said, it is an automatic response — "If I find myself starting to slip into the lower throat, I'll try to hop back up."

And the spasticity has not returned.

So much of what I read in print is appalling to me. Information that is grossly false and misleading. These are not Johnny-come-lately publications or tabloids, but honorable newspapers, magazines and journals that are known for their accuracy and high standards. For example, in 1989, the prestigious *New York Times* health guru Jane Brody, known in some circles as "the most trusted voice in health," wrote in her column that "one voice disorder, Spastic Dysphonia, has no known cure."

Because that statement is so blatantly incorrect, I wrote to Ms. Brody. In my letter to her, I told of patients who have recovered from SD by Direct Voice

Rehabilitation. The patients were purposely listed by name (with their permission) as their "before" and "after" diagnosis had been verified by ENT doctors.

I did not hear from Jane Brody or the *New York Times*. Because of their silence and unwillingness to print a more objective (and correct) view in her column, and because I believed so wholeheartedly that the truth should be told, I took space in the American Speech-Language-Hearing Association's monthly journal, *Asha*. It was my intent to run my letter to Jane Brody as an Open Letter in a full-page ad under the heading.

"A Response by a Voice and Speech Pathologist
to the *New York Times* 'Personal Health'
Column Written by Jane Brody"

ASHA would not accept the ad as submitted. Would I be willing to forward a revised version or substitute another ad? My answer was "no" since the Brody statement needed addressing. Janet Ciuccio, Director of the Professional Ethics Division of ASHA, remained firm. The ad could not run "as is," because portions of its wording were found to be objectionable.

Two months later, in its November 1989 issue, my Open Letter ad to Jane Brody made its way into the pages of *Asha*. Despite my protests, and offer to submit documented evidence, three paragraphs had been deleted. The censored paragraphs presented positive proof of my successes with patients using Direct Voice Rehabilitation. To make matters worse, ASHA refused to openly acknowledge that the ad had been censored and why until months later. Only after an angry exchange did ASHA finally admit the elimination of paragraphs containing valuable and relevant documentation.

It is unfortunate that the prevailing views of some

practitioners in medicine can so influence, even dictate, how speech pathologists learn and respond to spastic or spasmodic dysphonia and other voice disorders. Speech pathologists should be the primary service providers for spasmodic dysphonia and other voice disorders. Reliance on the medical model has not worked. However, speech pathologists depend on M.D.'s for referrals, and therefore may take a deferential position. The medical model in the treatment of voice disorders, especially spasmodic dysphonia, is wide of the mark with a number of patients. As a matter of record, when I was on staff, and later a clinical assistant professor on the medical faculty, at UCLA Medical Center from 1962 to 1969, we never had one success with spasmodic dysphonia using the medical model. But as a single practitioner and in private practice, I have been successful for the past 20 years.

AN ON-GOING CONTROVERSY

The prevailing views were on display at a Symposium ("Understanding and Treatment for Spasmodic Dysphonia. . . "), sponsored by the Department of Neurology at the University of California, Irvine, in March of 1991. During the meeting, the audience and the panel, which included Dr. Herb Dedo, "suggested . . . that at present there is no cure for SD," according to a newsletter dedicated to those with spasmodic dysphonia, entitled *Our Voice* (Nov. 1991), p. 2. As a member of this audience, I took exception, during this meeting, specifically recalling one patient, the Reverend James Johnson, who recovered within one month of intensive therapy using my Direct Voice Rehabilitation. Following that, I said, the Reverend Johnson continued therapy on his own and has maintained the right voice, an excellent voice, ever since. I also discussed recoveries and cures of other patients. No mention of my comments appeared in this newsletter.

In the same issue of this newsletter (p. 2), it was reported that "Dr. Dedo suggested that voice therapy may well be effective, but that it is difficult for patients to continue with the rigorous demands of speech pattern modification exercises."

I wish I had heard Dr. Dedo make these comments at the meeting.

The editor of *Our Voice*, apparently thinks I am controversial. I am not sure if her opinion is of me or my methods used to reverse wrong voices. Either way she might be right. The same may be said of any number of advances and breakthroughs, as well as those who pioneered them. Through the years, progress and controversy have gone hand in hand.

Still, I find it difficult to understand why a newsletter devoted to providing information about a debilitating voice condition, including the latest happenings in the field relating to it, almost always ignores my name and my work. Meanwhile, the newsletter hammers home the myths that there are no successes with voice therapy in articles by-lined by different sources, mainly medical people and speech pathologists. As far as *Our Voice* is concerned, my successes with spastic or spasmodic dysphonia by Direct Voice Rehabilitation seem not to exist.

WHAT'S GOING ON?

Another meeting took place at the Pacific Voice Conference, held in San Francisco during October, 1991. This Conference did not recognize the contribution of Direct Voice Therapy for SD. Instead, the stress was on Botox poison; not once did I hear anyone remind us of a leading doctor's statement at Irvine — withdraw Botox at the earliest possible time — or was I hearing things at the Irvine meeting and did he not recommend Botox be replaced?

A top authority suggested the Isshiki surgical procedure (mentioned previously) that can help a person move from a normal to a professional voice. From my experience, a professional, artistic voice cannot be created by a surgery.

One of the most interesting comments came from Dr. Arnold Aronson of the Mayo Clinic. He said he supported the position that I had produced recoveries with psychological cases of SD. (He separates SD into psychogenic and neurological cases, among other categories.) I do not find SD to be neurological; I find it to be a mechanical problem (voice misuse), with psychological overtones.

Recently, I received a copy of a letter written by Dr. Aronson that indicates he supports my techniques in psychogenic SD cases. The original was addressed to Lawrence Kolasa, President of the National Spasmodic Dysphonia Association (NSDA).

With all due respect to the various treatments for SD, I feel SD patients should also be informed about Direct Voice Rehabilitation. Incidentally, although NSDA states that they do not endorse any specific drug or treatment for SD, in NSDA's Spring 1994 Quarterly Report, they thanked Allergan Laboratories for a

$15,000.00 grant. As previously mentioned, Allergan Pharmaceuticals in 1990 acquired the substance that produces botulinum toxin.

A VOICE IN THE WILDERNESS?

Since I have had success in helping patients with spasmodic dysphonia, I want to persuade physicians and voice pathologists to try my techniques. But I feel as though mine is a voice crying in the wilderness. The only way I know to announce that spasmodic dyphonia may be helped by Direct Voice Rehabilitation is to let patients who have recovered from spasmodic dysphonia tell their stories, and I can only hope that other voice pathologists will help other patients.

I have devoted my long career to bring the field of voice rehabilitation out of obscurity and to the attention of the public — to tell everyone that there is help for misused and abused voices, for voice disorders, and for people who want to improve their speaking voices.

I have used every means possible to publicize voice rehabilitation. I have written articles, chapters, and books. I have given many radio and television interviews. I have made speeches and conducted seminars. I have been fortunate that some celebrity patients I have helped have allowed me to use their names in an attempt to make voice rehabilitation vocally visible to the general public. Quietly doing voice rehabilitation and being successful will help a few, but in order to get many patients with voice problems to seek help from professionals in this field, voice and speech pathology must be publicized.

After many years of attempting to educate, I felt

that the Open Letter approach for relaying information was in order. The Brody letter brought added attention to spasmodic dysphonia, but it seems obvious the field of voice and speech pathology does not want attention. Nor does it care to listen to the recoveries or discuss them.

The spasmodic dysphonic patients, whose case histories report recoveries and cures, were diagnosed by notable and knowledgeable laryngologists and by leading medical centers, including Stanford University, Mayo Clinic, and UCLA, among others. There are those in academia and medicine who are of the view that recoveries and cures from SD involving DVR are anecdotal and without independent confirmation or independent verification. These are proven, documented cases of patients who *had* SD with follow-up reports to show the successful treatment producing a normal voice by DVR, a *special* therapy that was developed and perfected over many years of practice.

Speech and voice pathologists throughout the country and around the world can do what I am doing. I simplify. They can, too. The public benefits. Direct Voice Rehabilitation has benefited many people and continues to do so.

And so I write these words not only to speak directly to readers experiencing problems with their voices which they wish to remedy, but also to speak to physicians, voice clinicians, and allied professionals in the hope they will expand their openness to Direct Voice Rehabilitation. If I am able to reach some colleagues and professionals, I will be gratified. Having success with afflicted patients has been and will continue to be my greatest satisfaction.

It is my fondest hope and dream that voice pathologists or clinicians will work with strangled voice patients using Direct Voice Rehabilitation. Patients who come to see me from different areas of the United States, as well as from other countries, often need on-going follow-up assistance, when they return home, to maintain the gains, progress, and/or recoveries they have made in my office. These patients need a support system of voice clinicians, physicians, other patients, and support groups, such as the NSDA, in order to continue the recovery progress. By working together we can all look forward to an orientation that is geared to recoveries and cures for strangled voices.

10

What You May Not Know About Voice And Speech

We change our voices throughout the day. Half the time we don't know it. Other times we think we're being silly. If you have a child at home, or a family pet, you know what I mean. Have you ever noticed how your voice changes when you talk to a baby or a pet? Your voice becomes warmer and more positive. That is because pets and babies humanize us. They break down our inhibitions and bring us back to ourselves, both in voice and in feelings.

PRACTICING "PET TALK"

"People talk" — that is, the way you talk to people — is often guarded and strained. "Pet talk," as I call it, is endearing, relaxed, and friendly. When you talk in this way, notice how the subject (pet or baby) becomes more responsive.

Imagine you have a pet with you now, and say a few words. Notice the soft, *natural* quality of your voice. While it may not have the correct pitch or tone focus, it does have a warmth and gentle persuasiveness you may want to use in your everyday conversations.

Pet talk illustrates our ability to use different voices for different situations. We all do that at various times each day. For instance, a businessman may use one voice with his associates and clients, and another at home. The same goes for doctors, attorneys, salespeople, teachers, and just about everyone else who deals with the public. Celebrities and politicians "play games" with their voices. Chances are, you do, too. Your voice changes with the roles you assume throughout the day. In the office you want to sound assured and assertive. At home, you are less cautious about the way you speak.

THE GAMES WE PLAY WITH OUR VOICES

Have you noticed that you use one voice on the phone when you're talking to a friend, and another with a stranger? You speak one way with an associate and another way with a superior. Do you sound the same when you call a family member as when you call for an appointment? You undoubtedly talk one way with men and another way with women, just as you do with children, babies and pets.

Most people play the voice game without realizing it. Depending on mood, pressures or environment, their voices change automatically. Some people, however, are quite aware of the game they are playing. In fact, they have become so good at it that they use their voices as weapons. You've heard those voices, and may even have been a target at times. It is the voice that lashes out, the voice that people use to make a point. Such a voice is often fierce and intimidating. But it is not always bombastic and sharp. It may also be more calculating, used to tempt and persuade. These voices are often harmful physically, because they come from the lower throat, pressing and straining. They not only irritate the speakers' throats but hurt their voices.

You may use different voices without pushing your voice or hurting yourself, by keeping your tone focus in the mask and using your natural pitch range. A different voice for different situations can be enjoyable as well as effective in helping to make a strong impression.

No matter where you are, at home or at work, your voice should be comfortable and give you confidence. That isn't always easy. In many older people, voice strain occurs all too frequently. The strain may become more than merely bothersome or annoying; it may become pressing enough to fatigue the speaking voice with only a few minutes of speech. It may also create laryngeal and pharyngeal tensions and troubles. These, in turn, may interfere with communication and lead to organic dysphonias, such as nodes, polyps, and contact ulcer.

THE GERIATRIC VOICE

The aging process affects the voice — pitch, quality, volume, and rate — in some people more than in others. The tired voice begins to falter and, at times, fail. The tone wavers and the volume decreases. The carrying power of the voice is reduced, sometimes markedly, and people ask, "What did you say?" more frequently. The intelligibility of speech lowers and diction becomes distorted. (Dentures may impair articulation.)

In some cases, as one ages, the voice deepens and

reaches its zenith, enriching it with the beauty of its potential. Ronald Reagan is an example of that kind of voice. In many older Americans, however, the aging process deteriorates the voice, which I find results from the ongoing wrong use of the speaking voice, culminating in a tired, fatigued voice that misrepresents us.

Physicians attribute the aging voice in the older patient to increasing age, genes, and neurological causes. I say in most cases it is due to the wrong use of voice, that is, whether the voice has been used too high or too low in pitch. Ronald Reagan had too high a pitch for years, but aging caused his voice to drop in pitch. Few of us are that lucky, and fewer realize we may change for the better at any time in our lives.

Voice strain and voice fatigue, or tired voice, are two of the basic signs and symptoms of voice misuse. Although a number of speakers experience it, few ever realize that such symptoms are produced by the speaker himself, and that the symptoms are merely nature's means and method of informing the person of the impending voice problem. At times, voice strain is temporary and may be due to use of the voice in noisy surroundings, perhaps from a noisy car or from cheering at a ball game.

AGE — OR VOICE MISUSE?

More often than not, however, voice strain is created by long-term voice misuse. The proof is that the problem occurs more and more frequently as the voice is used, with fewer and fewer periods of ease and comfort. But the voice need not always be affected by aging. Bob Hope is the perfect example of that. We age the voice by voice misuse and abuse.

Voice strain that creates voice difficulties or voice fatigue is often responsive to Direct Voice Rehabilitation. The symptoms respond to voice training and disappear when the patient learns to produce a voice that is natural and appropriate.

The tired voice of many geriatric patients may be attended to with Direct Voice Rehabilitation within a short period of time if the patient cooperates. Voice misuse basically is due to a wrong pitch and focus of voice (usually too low and in the lower throat) and poor habits for speech. Generally, some ear training and a directed new pitch level and tone focus, as well as midsection breath control are given the patient.

Geriatric patients who have organic lesions, such as nodes, polyps, or contact ulcer on the vocal folds, or bowed vocal folds, may also be able to overcome such conditions with voice rehabilitation. The lesions actually disappear with correct voice usage. Even patients who have had surgery performed on their larynx may be helped to speak again, easily and comfortably by Direct Voice Rehabilitation.

OTHER FACTORS THAT MAY AFFECT ELDERLY VOICES

One of the most prominent voice problems is that of Parkinson's disease. The voice may be affected, and the severity may increase with time. With voice rehabilitation, the voice may be strengthened for many of these patients who have the desire and determination to improve their voices. Speaking at a Parkinsonian Support Group lately, I demonstrated how patients with slurred and unintelligible speech and voices were able to produce clear and efficient voices.

Factors which may contribute to a wrong voice are increased body fatigue, which results in less air pressure to the lungs and a subsequent drop in pitch; emotions, such as grief, despair and resignation that create use of lower pitch levels; and a present or previous voice image, which is that sound or voice that attracts or repels. The aging voice may be changed from an effortful voice that uses a throaty, tired tone with throat irritation to an easy voice with a clear tone and no irritation. Vitamins or relevant medications must be continued, if required, or the patient will be physically unable to perform or produce the new, healthier voice.

A voice image often exists in the geriatric patient, although the need for the male to produce a low voice (for authority and masculinity) is of less importance at this time of life. Nor is it as important for the female to seek a sexy, low-pitched voice.

Unfortunately, many aging patients who complain of voice fatigue or tired voice are left to their own devices and solutions. Some patients use lozenges to cope with the problem, but lozenges offer only minimal relief and are not a real solution. The throat irritation may be temporarily alleviated, but after the person talks for a time, the irritation and pain return. Lozenges may merely mask the pain without removing it. Throat sprays, gargles, pills, and vitamins are also commonly used, but, as with the lozenges, they are basically ineffective since they deal with the symptom and not the cause.

HOW THE VOICE MAY REACT TO MEDICATIONS

Medications pose another problem, and not only for the elderly. They may contain a relaxant, which causes lack of energy and drowsiness. I recall a gentleman who came to my office because he was losing his voice. After explaining how to reverse his condition, I asked him to place his voice in the mask. He tried, but he had a difficult time. When I asked if he was on medication, he admitted that he had been taking a Valium-like substance. The medication was actually contributing to his voice problem by bringing, and keeping, his voice down.

Another patient had been taking an antispasmodic drug to combat spasms of the vocal cords. Yet the drug, which was to control the spasms, actually added to them whenever he tried to talk.

Lack of sleep may also hinder therapy. A tired patient will have difficulty obtaining a voice lift, that is, taking the voice from the lower throat and placing it in the mask.

With medication, when relevant, and with a good night's sleep, a tired voice in the geriatric patient may be amenable to voice rehabilitation with a relatively brief period of therapy. However, a cooperative link must exist between the family physician, internist, laryngologist, and voice specialist for the patient to receive fast and permanent results.

Most people may speak easily, if not clearly, at any age, but they aren't aware (or convinced) that their tired voices may be made comfortable and healthy. Therefore, because of ignorance, misdirection or disbelief, many geriatric patients needlessly suffer voice disorders. No matter what your age, if you are using your voice correctly, there is no reason to lose your voice until you draw your last breath, barring a severe medical problem affecting the voice. In fact, there is no reason not to have a feel-good, sound-good voice that communicates who you are to the world.

THE "LAZY" VOICE

Tired voices, particularly in the geriatric patient, should not be confused with "lazy voice." I wasn't familiar with that term "lazy voice" until I heard it from one of my acquaintances at the gym. He came to me one day to tell me he was having trouble with his throat. He also mentioned that his voice was weak and didn't carry. I told him he needed a voice lift; he was talking from his lower throat. "Bring your voice up," I said. "That will take the pressure off your throat. Your voice will carry and it won't tire."

He didn't know where to place his voice until he tried my Instant Voice Press. Then he could hear and *feel* his natural placement.

When he spoke again, his voice was stronger. "I don't have a lazy voice anymore," he said, sounding surprised at how simple the change had been. "And I'm not mumbling. Maybe it won't be so hard for people to understand me now. My voice had been buried in my throat."

A voice lift was all it took.

STUTTERING

For older people with problem voices, speaking can be so effortful, painful, and traumatic that they sometimes simply stop talking and live in a voiceless world. The same can be said for anyone who suffers from a severe voice problem or the person who stutters. Actually, I liken stuttering more to SD, because the field, I believe, offers the same prognosis: no cures (another myth, as I see it). Maybe that is because, like SD, stuttering is being treated on the basis of reducing the symptoms, not curing the problem.

The real problem may lie with some people who work with stutterers, those gurus in the field of stuttering who are stutterers themselves. Maybe they are saying stuttering is incurable because they remain stutterers. I may make you better, they say. *Better is not well.* Whatever happened to the credo, "Physician heal thyself?" If they aren't able to do that, how may they help others? I say stop looking for outside influences and excuses. Stop treating the symptoms and start curing.

LIVING WITH FALSE SPEECH IMAGES

Stutterers live with false speech images, long settled and terribly defeating. Stutterers believe they must speak perfectly when they talk. Being "perfect" is a stutterer's big obstacle. In seeking perfection of speech, he strives to impress, not knowing that seeking perfection only adds to the stuttering.

Stutterers feel they must talk without hesitation, prolongation, repetition and fillers, such as "ahhs," "umms," and other normal bobbles. With that in mind, talking becomes stressful. Stutterers tense up and do all the things they believe they shouldn't do. Thus, stutterers avoid the normal things we all do — like hemming and hawing, repeating a sound or word, mispronouncing a word, inserting vocal sighs, and using "uhs," "ahs," and "umms."

Many people start by saying "well . . ." and sprinkling "you know" or "I mean" into a conversation. These conversational aids, which I call "fillers," are unacceptable to stutterers. They think of how they are going to talk before they talk. Worse, they think about the words and sounds not coming out right. Trying to be perfect fails because perfection is impossible, and striving for perfection makes for perfect stuttering.

While stutterers try for perfection in speech, non-stutterers simply say what they feel, hoping for the best. Non-stutterers may think ahead, but not of speech sounds. This preoccupation with sound actually contributes to the problem, because stutterers mechanically and artificially preset their speech mechanism by forcing the tongue against the roof of the mouth or upper teeth, or tightening the lips, so the sound can come out easily. By doing that, however, they stop the free flow of the tongue and lips, and make the mouth a battleground for keeping sounds in and holding back the natural flow of speech in synergy. Stutterers all too often hold their breath, reverse their breathing, or try to talk without air.

Of interest is realizing normal talkers use hand movement or hand gestures naturally to express themselves. Stutterers use these hand movements and gestures artificially to get the words out and to continue the flow of speech.

ON BEING AN IMPERFECT SPEAKER

How do you get stutterers to stop stuttering? By changing their orientation, their thought process. By making them realize *there are no perfect speakers.* There never were, never will be.

Stutterers do not hear imperfections in normal speaking patterns of others. One important aspect of therapy is to have stutterers become aware of imperfections in the speech of others. To do this, tape record non-professional speakers on radio, on TV, or in person, and later listen for, and tally, imperfections, such as "ah," "well," "you know," etc. in the speech of normal, off-the-cuff talkers.

The stuttering pattern may be broken by distractions. Shake a stutterer's hand and he/she momentarily becomes a normal talker. Hand shaking or any distraction takes the mind off speech sounds and lets nature take its course. Speaking should be spontaneous and automatic, and stutterers are not spontaneous when talking, let alone automatic; stutterers are on manual, self-monitoring themselves for feared sounds. That may also be said of many non-stutterers, but they cover those split-second, thought-searching lulls with fillers and "bobbles." Bobbles are what we all do in speech — hesitate, repeat a word or sound, prolong a word or sound. It is okay to bobble. It is okay to pause and not say every word perfectly. Stuttering stops the flow; bobbling lets it be. Stutterers won't accept that — or they try not to — and so they stutter.

WANTING TO SOUND GOOD

I recall a patient, Jason, who replied when I asked why he stuttered: "Because I want to look good, and sound good." Jason admitted that he tried to impress, especially when speaking in public or with an important person in his life. He also admitted that when he talked aloud to himself, he talked without stuttering. That was because, Jason said, he wasn't trying to impress himself. Stutterers may also be able to talk to pets without stuttering for the same reason; they are not trying to impress.

I wanted Jason to talk that way always, as if he were talking aloud to himself. "The harder I try, the worse it gets," he said. Jason didn't hear the imperfections as other people spoke to him. He never heard the bobbles. If he did, he certainly didn't want them in his speech. He wanted perfection, believing that perfection is "normal."

In public speaking, I have found that the person who tries hard to impress does worse than the person who simply talks. The best speakers say what they have to say, as if talking to a pal.

I once asked Jason if talking for him was natural or artificial. His answer was "artificial."

"If it isn't natural," I inquired, "then who, or what, is creating the stuttering?"

"I am," he replied. "I push to get the speech out, wanting to get over the stuttering. It doesn't work so I react to it, which compounds the problem. How do I stop stuttering?"

I told Jason to gradually undo the tongue and the lip stance. "Get the feel of it when it happens, and contrast it to the relaxed state of your tongue and lips when you're not trying to talk. Practice making them tense when you're alone and relaxed. Feel them tense, then relaxed. Tense . . . then relaxed. Get to know and *feel* the difference. Don't rush. Give yourself plenty of space and time to undo the wrong. Practice and speaking will become more natural and normal. And don't be afraid to bobble. Bobbling is part of talking naturally. Everybody does it."

THE "STAGE FRIGHT" SYNDROME

Stutterers are forever afraid of talking, fearing they won't talk well. When they do try to communicate they actually show a physiological difference from the person who speaks normally.

I have worked with stutterers successfully by getting them to change their orientation and to realize that speaking is not difficult. They have simply made it difficult. When I was Director of the Adult Stutterers' Group at Stanford University, outstanding successes were achieved by changing the orientation of the stutterers' concept of normal speech and by practicing what is normal.

There are also similarities between stutterers, spasmodic dysphonics, and people who have stage fright. With stutterers and SD patients, it is a perpetual case of stage fright. The pressure is constant. The very thought of speaking creates stress, fear, and anxiety.

Stutterers may be successful talkers. But making it happen requires putting aside all ideas of perfection, which make speaking laborious and painful. The slight imperfections in our speech patterns actually help make us human and give us a personality that is uniquely our own.

11

How to Get a Voice That Really Talks for You

God bless Bill Clinton. His hoarse voice has been a blessing in disguise for opening a real discussion about voices. That is something many in the medical field have been able to avoid until now.

To read all the conflicting advice offered by doctors, one would think these doctors may not know what they are doing. One says "do this"; the other says "do that." They all have their own definite opinions as to what are workable procedures, some as ridiculous as chewing on a golf ball, avoiding dry rooms, and taking warm showers to relax the throat muscles.

I have long been at odds with the medical profession on these procedures and others, specifically those relating to spasmodic dysphonia, a condition considered hopeless by the doctors, as well as most speech pathologists. Their treatment of spasmodic dysphonia is to contain the symptoms, not to cure the problem.

According to current reports in medical and speech pathology literature, the suggested area of the disorder is the basal ganglia of the brain. In other words, the condition is thought to be neurological. Others believe the condition to be genetically related. I disagree markedly with the theory of genetic and neurological causations, finding the cause to be mechanical — voice misuse and abuse — with psychological overtones. I also disagree that spastic or spasmodic dysphonia is "hopeless." Over the past 20 years, I have documented success — cures and recoveries — with Direct Voice Rehabilitation that totally destroy that theory.

A patient may have a neurological problem, such as cerebral palsy, and SD as well, but the SD is not necessarily caused by the cerebral palsy. One patient with cerebral palsy had no voice problem until he had a severe cold. Following the cold, the voice problem that had begun during the cold continued, eventuating into SD. His physician said his voice problem was due to his neurological problem, namely, cerebral palsy. The patient said his physician did not understand that the voice problem began during the cold, and that he had not had a voice problem before the cold.

Another patient was diagnosed by her physician as having SD due to a neurological problem, namely "a mini-stroke." She did recover her normal voice through direct voice rehabilitation.

A CONCLUSIVE STUDY

As early as 1973, I conducted a study and analysis at the UCLA Medical Center involving 155 patients. These patients underwent voice rehabilitation for 14 types of medically diagnosed functional and organic dysphonias, including nodules, contact ulcers, polyps, bowed vocal cords, paralytic dysphonia, spastic (or spasmodic) dysphonia, falsetto voice, weak or tired voice (wrong voice), and incipient spastic dysphonia (a less severe form of spastic or spasmodic dysphonia, and frequently a forerunner of either spastic or spasmodic dysphonia). The ages of the adult patients, men and women, ranged from 15 to 73 years. Three boys were of ages 13, 12, and 11, with the conditions of contact ulcer, nodules, and wrong voice, respectively.

The purpose of the study was to evaluate the relationship between pitch and hoarseness in dysphonia. Although some writers, prior to the study, had discussed hoarseness as a major deviant quality found in patients with voice disorders, and a correlation between hoarseness and lower pitch level had been noted, few clinicians had attempted an objective evaluation before and after therapy.

The results of this study were conclusive. Of the 155 dysphonic patients, 150 had been using too low a pitch before therapy. The pitch was raised to the optimal or natural pitch level with balanced oral and nasal resonance (mask focus). Diaphragmatic or midsection breath support was developed. The patients were also afforded *voice* psychotherapy to help them adjust to a new sound and voice image, since nearly all had a wrong voice image. After therapy, the patients were basically free of hoarseness. A follow-up of 128 of these 155 patients indicated that three months to seven years after the completion of voice therapy, 98 percent of the 128 patients had remained good or excellent,which is a remarkable success ratio. The study also confirmed that the use of a pitch which is below the optimal or natural level is a major factor in contributing to or in continuing most types of dysphonias.

Of late, the treatment of severely troubled voices is being pursued by aggressive medicine, and aggressive intervention, with injections of botulinum toxin or surgery. These practices carry risk factors and, in general, simply abate some of the symptoms while ignoring the cause. Medicine acknowledges its symptomatic treatment of spasmodic or spastic dysphonia, and voices in general.

One of my ear-nose-throat colleagues referred a patient, saying that seventy to eighty percent of all benign growths do not need surgery; they can be eliminated through direct voice rehabilitation. Interestingly enough, when the patient is a famous singer, or a well-known star, surgery may be contraindicated since the quality of voice may be adversely affected.

GETTING BACK TO BASICS

Physicians need to go back to basics. They need to listen to voices and make their diagnoses by ear as well as by visual symptoms. They need to relate hoarse voices to possible misuse of voice, not just to a medical cause and medical treatment. The cure to a hoarse voice may lie in changing the wrong voice to the right voice.

I try to help people to learn how to use the voice easily and well so that they can talk without the use of hormones, steroids, drugs, surgery, and Botox to help the voice. (Hormones, steroids, medication, and surgery, when relevant, are appropriate care for *medical* conditions.) I try to help the patient with a troubled voice find that the voice is not a complicated instrument, but rather a simple mechanism that takes some learning and practice to use well and efficiently. This way the patient can take control of the voice without me or others and have a voice that is well used.

KEEPING IT SIMPLE

What I do is no mystery. It is simple, maybe too simple for some to accept. In a nutshell, I help you find your right, natural voice, and then help you to keep it.

My credo has always been to "keep it simple." Life is already too complicated, and time is much too precious. Medicine needs to simplify, to make what is generally perceived as difficult easy to understand.

One of the easiest, least complicated procedures is to make a wrong voice right, a sick voice healthy again. The field may not agree, but to me, it is as simple as 1, 2, 3. The magic is within you — given a simple right direction and competent hands-on by Direct Voice Rehabilitation, as I see it. My goal is to help you develop your voice into a user-friendly, listener-friendly voice.

A NON-RISK APPROACH TO VOICES

My approach to all types of voice disorders, as well as to improving the speaking voice from a normal to a professional sound, is the same. It is a non-risk, non-invasive, non-medical approach, one that is in keeping with the tradition of the medical creed, *Do No Harm*, while helping people talk again with a normal, healthy voice.

Direct Voice Rehabilitation is not speech therapy or the usual voice therapy. It is a new approach I originated and developed and hope many others will adopt and practice for treating voice disorders and all types of voices; this approach emphasizes the variables of pitch, tone focus, and breath support which are the variables that affect and control quality of voice and volume.

Each voice has a natural or optimal pitch level at which an individual gets the most amount of sound for the least amount of effort. In addition to the optimal pitch level, there is the habitual pitch level. This is the pitch level the person uses from day to day. These two pitch levels, optimal and habitual, should be the same. But too often the habitual pitch is not at the optimal or natural pitch level. If your habitual pitch level is too far above or below the optimal pitch level, you are misusing your voice.

Closely related to the pitch level is the tone focus, or resonance, in the voice. The resonance of the voice comes from three areas: the upper throat or nose, the middle throat or mouth, and the lower throat (the area around the larynx or voice box). There should be a balance of resonance in these three areas. When the voice is correctly placed, the voice has a buzz or ring that centers around the mouth and nose, the mask area.

A very simple way to check your pitch level and tone focus is to say "um-hmm" naturally and spontaneously as though agreeing with someone. Then say "um-hmm . . . one," "um-hmm . . . two." Is the pitch of the "um-hmm" at the same pitch level as the numbers? If they are approximately the same level, chances are you are using the correct pitch.

A back-up method to check your habitual pitch and tone focus is to place one hand on the chest and the other hand on the stomach and breathe in with your stomach moving out. Then, keeping your lips closed, make a humming sound and press in on the stomach in a quick staccato fashion. (This is my Instant Voice Press, as noted earlier in Chapter 2.) The sound escapes through the nose, and you will feel a buzz around the mouth and nose, or the mask area. Talking with resonance in the mask gives the voice a clear and efficient sound. You may talk easily and comfortably throughout the day without tiring your voice.

LISTENING IS ESSENTIAL

Despite the extreme severity in some problem voices, such as spastic and spasmodic dysphonia, it is still possible in most cases to hear and locate the correct optimal pitch level and range quickly. Listening to the speaking voice is essential to realizing that the tone focus in spastic or spasmodic dysphonia is always coming from the lower throat.

Spasmodic dysphonia and spastic dysphonia are not the beginning or early symptom of a wrong voice. More often than not, it is the end or the completion of a cycle of misuse that usually begins with a hoarse voice, a tired voice, fatigue of voice or effortful voice that may move through nodes, polyps or contact ulcers of the larynx. In fact, I have noticed that some of my patients with SD have had such growths before getting SD or at the same time they experienced SD.

Bowed vocal cords are also basically produced from the wrong pitch, incorrect focus of the voice, poor breath support, and/or an inept voice image, but can occur at times from intubation. Although this condition, in general, is considered to be neurological in cause, I find it to be essentially functional and mechanical in nature. That is, the individual is misusing the speaking voice, talking from the lower throat with an inappropriate pitch level and poor breath support.

I am reminded of a patient from San Francisco who

had been diagnosed by a Bay Area research facility as having bowed vocal cords. He was to be scheduled for a surgical procedure on the superior laryngeal nerve, enervating the vocal cord and larynx to correct the problem, when he came to me. I listened to the young man, and it was obvious to me that he had functionally created bowed vocal cords from voice misuse. Within a couple of sessions he had his voice back. When he returned to San Francisco his ENT confirmed that his "bowed vocal cords were going away" by his change of voice from a deep-throat low pitch to optimal pitch and mask focus.

In seeking voice rehabilitation, the ear of the clinician is the key to directing the procedure. The clinician must know what to listen for to locate and secure the optimal pitch level and range as well as a balanced tone focus. A person who is trained in voice must know how to *listen.*

Direct Voice Rehabilitation is similar for all types of voice disorders and voice improvement. I find that almost all types of voice patients have in common the misuse or poor use of pitch, tone focus and/or breath support. They also have the wrong voice image of what is right in voice. The voice image must be addressed directly and openly, or else the patient will pursue the correct mechanical variables but will not pursue the correct voice.

PROGNOSIS: GOOD TO EXCELLENT

I believe and find that the prognosis for almost all problem voices, including spastic and spasmodic dysphonia, is good to excellent. But the patients must be cooperative. As I noted earlier, some patients are simply more gifted than others, some are more willing to change than others, and some are so resistant to change they will never recover.

But don't let me mislead you. Not everyone has a severe voice problem. Many people simply want to improve their voices by making them more pleasing and listenable. And that too is part of voice fitness.

For anyone with a voice problem, it is important to know this: YOU ARE NOT ALONE. Medical intervention may have failed you, but hopeless may not be hopeless at all. DO NOT GIVE UP.

If you do want to improve your voice, start by finding your natural voice. You may do this in only seconds, but it takes practice to keep it. Practice is not something you have to do. It is something you want to do because you want to better your voice and your life. By practicing you have the chance to learn how to identify, locate and establish your right voice, the one you want to represent you at your very best.

WHAT YOUR VOICE SAYS ABOUT YOU

It is no secret that when you speak with a tired voice you generally come across as a weak or vulnerable person. Conversely, a strong, healthy voice gives you a more confident, forceful and dynamic persona.

The majority of adults have poor or tired voices, but we weren't born that way. Nearly all of us were born with the ability to have "star quality" voices. As we grew older, however, we began to misuse and abuse this God-given gift. We began to lose our voices — and we didn't know it. As long as our voices worked, and we could communicate, we believed everything was fine. It wasn't until you heard yourself on a recorder that you knew something was wrong. Or perhaps your voice began to falter or fail, sounding hoarse and scratchy. Then you *really* knew something was wrong.

Part of the problem is that we rarely hear ourselves as we are. We think we sound better than we do, until we actually hear ourselves. We also have different voices for different occasions and different people. All too often we let our emotions and feelings speak for us. Haven't you found that it is easy to "read" a person just by the sound of his or her voice? You can almost always tell whether that person is happy, sad, apprehensive, angry, tired, not feeling well, or whatever. Then, again, you may *think* a person's voice — even your own — is implying one thing and the reverse is true. How many times has a friend asked, "Do you feel all right? You sound tired." Your reply may very well have been: "I'm fine. I feel great."

Isn't it time you let your voice really speak for you? Get your voice back on track by talking in the mask, around your lips and nose. That's the area that makes your voice so likable and listenable, and allows you to talk without fatigue. All good and great voices talk on the buzz.

Voice fitness care is simple to do, if you have the right direction. Learning a new voice requires that you hear, feel and sense it in the mask. If you now talk too low in pitch or let your voice stay in the lower one-third of your throat (the lower throat around your voice box), try my basic exercises for starters.

A CLOSING REVIEW

Let's review them one more time.
Say "um-hmm" naturally and spontaneously and

feel the buzz, the tingle of your voice around your mouth and nose. Then try adding "um-hmm . . . one," the "one" being at the same pitch and focus as the "hmm" sound. Then, throughout the day, when you're alone, instead of thinking thoughts, "hmm" them to yourself. That is called *private practice.* Next, match the words to the "hmm."

In order to practice while communicating with others, simply affirm hearing them by saying "um-hmm" gently and easily in agreement, which we all like to hear. The "hmming" allows you to focus on your voice throughout the day. This is *public practice.*

Again, let me remind you: Another way to find your right voice is to use my Instant Voice Press. (Remember — do not attempt this exercise if you are pregnant or have stomach problems.) Take a finger and gently jiggle it at the solar plexus — the bottom of the breast bone — keeping your mouth closed and letting the voice come forth on a "hmm" as you gently but persistently press on the area. You should find a resonance around your lips and nose, and that is where you should focus your voice to talk.

Don't forget correct breathing. Are you now breathing from the stomach or from the chest? Put one hand on your chest and the other hand on your stomach. Breathe in through your mouth and see what happens. Does your chest move? Rise? If so, you are breathing incorrectly for speech. You are lifting a weight. Your chest is composed of cartilage, bone, and muscles, and if you lift the rib cage (which you are doing when you feel it rise), you are basically lifting a weight eight to 12 times per minute. It is a weight you don't need or want, a weight that fatigues your body from the continued effort to lift the weight throughout the day. When you breathe from the midsection or stomach, you have flexibility and real control of your voice and volume.

These exercises are quite simple, yet they may help you find your natural voice, and relocate it whenever you are in doubt. Practice for seconds at a time throughout the day until your new, healthier voice becomes second nature to you. If you have problems understanding or using these exercises, or if you have a serious problem with your voice, such as vocal fold growths, a paralyzed vocal fold, bowed vocal folds, or spasmodic dysphonia, seek professional help from a competent voice clinician. Additionally, if you have a voice that continues to be fatigued or lacks strength or if you have continued raspiness or hoarseness, go for a medical check-up. Discuss your voice problem with your physician and request information so that you have options and alternatives for appropriate care.

THE IMPORTANCE OF A HEALTHY VOICE

A strong, healthy voice is important in today's competitive society. Such a voice enhances rather than detracts each time you speak. It not only represents you in a most pleasant, positive and powerful way, but lets you enjoy the give and take of conversation without a hint of hoarseness or voice fatigue, which may lead to more serious voice problems.

Are you listening, Mr. President?

References

—— "Chronic Voice Disorders," *Mayo Clinic Health Letter*, 11, 2 (February 1993), 1.

—— "Let's Talk," *ASHA*, 35, 11 (November 1993), 65.

—— "Pioneer In the Development of Botulinum Toxin," *Our Voice* (Fall 1992), 4.

—— *Discover* (August 1992), 92-33.

—— *Our Voice* (November 1991), 2, 4.

—— *Vital Signs*, 4 (1993), 40.

Altman, Lawrence, "Laryngitis Like Clinton's is Common Among Politicians," *The New York Times* (April 14, 1992).

Beyette, Beverly, "At Odds With Establishment: Therapist Talks Up Voice Makeovers," *The Los Angeles Times* (July 11, 1984), View, 1.

Brody, Jane E. "Personal Health: Vocal Short Circuit," *The New York Times* (March 11, 1992).

Brodnitz, Friedrich. *Vocal Rehabilitation.* 2nd ed. Rochester, Minnesota: Whiting Press, 1961.

Cooper, Morton. *Winning With Your Voice.* Hollywood, FL: Frederick Fell Publishers, Inc., 1989.

Cooper, Morton. *Change Your Voice, Change Your Life.* New York: Macmillan Publishing Company, 1984. Paperback--New York: Harper Collins, Publishers, 1985.

Cooper, Morton. *Modern Techniques of Vocal Rehabilitation.* Springfield, IL: Charles C Thomas, 1973.

Cooper, Morton. "Recovery from Spastic Dysphonia by Direct Voice Rehabilitation," *Proceedings of the 18th Congress of the International Association of Logopedics and Phoniatrics,* 1 (August 1980), 579-584.

Cooper, Morton. "Treating Spasmodic Dysphonia With Direct Voice Rehabilitation," *Advance* (February 1, 1993), 6-7.

Greene, Margaret C.L. and Lesley Mathieson. *The Voice and Its Disorders.* 5th ed. San Diego: Singular Publishing Group, Inc., 1989.

Hines, Jerome. *Great Singers on Great Singing.* New York: Doubleday, 1982.

Prelutsky, Burt, "Voice of Experience," *The Los Angeles Times* (September 1976), Calendar.

Sansweet, Stephen. "How Norton Simon, With Help, Finally Found Voice He Had Lost," *The Wall Street Journal,* CII, 64 (April 1, 1980), 1.

Segell, Michael. "Health Memo: News From the Medical World,"*Cosmopolitan* (October 1993), 66.

Sperling, Dan. "Is your voice hoarse? It could be just talk," *USA Today* (October 22, 1985), 2A.

Vaughan, Charles W. "Current Concepts in Otolaryngology. Diagnosis and Treatment of Organic Voice Disorder," *The New England Journal of Medicine*, 307 (1982), 863-866.

Dr. Cooper's private practice is located in the Brentwood section of Los Angeles at 11661 San Vicente Blvd., Suite 301, Los Angeles, CA 90049. For information concerning voice improvement audio and video cassettes, phone (800) 932-3221. For information about voice disorders, including the strangled voice (spasmodic dysphonia), for assistance in ordering the audio and video cassettes ("Cures and Recoveries from Spastic and Spasmodic Dysphonia"), and for general information, as well as for books and articles, phone (310) 208-6047 or fax (310) 207-6769.

NOTES

NOTES

NOTES